Madhuja Mukherjee's new compilation of diverse writings and images of women from the early cinema revisits well-known archival resources with new historical concerns and opens up entirely new archival resources. Although there has been work done on stardom and women in the early cinema, the complexity of the 'gender' question, especially as it might relate to texts produced by the stars themselves, in poetry, letters and in interviews—and on occasion in valuable autobiographies—is nowhere near exhausted. This compilation will go alongside Mukherjee's well-known teachings, writings, installations and her forays into film practice to open a new dimension to a very under-discussed and under-researched area of film history.

Ashish Rajadhyaksha,
an eminent film studies scholar and cultural critic,
Centre for the Study of Culture and Society, Bengaluru

VOICES OF THE
TALKING STARS

VOICES OF THE TALKING STARS
Women of Indian Cinema and Beyond

Edited by
Madhuja Mukherjee

School of Women's Studies, Jadavpur University

Los Angeles | London | New Delhi
Singapore | Washington DC | Melbourne

First published in 2017 by

SAGE Publications India Pvt Ltd
B1/I-1 Mohan Cooperative Industrial Area
Mathura Road, New Delhi 110 044, India
www.sagepub.in

STREE
16 Southern Avenue
Kolkata 700 026
www.stree-samyabooks.com

SAGE Publications Inc
2455 Teller Road
Thousand Oaks, California 91320, USA

SAGE Publications Ltd
1 Oliver's Yard, 55 City Road
London EC1Y 1SP, United Kingdom

SAGE Publications Asia-Pacific Pte Ltd
3 Church Street
#10-04 Samsung Hub
Singapore 049483

Published by Vivek Mehra for SAGE Publications India Pvt Ltd, typeset in 11/13 pt Baskerville SSi by Zaza Eunice, Hosur, Tamil Nadu, India and printed at Saurabh Printers Pvt Ltd, Greater Noida.

Library of Congress Cataloging-in-Publication Data Available

ISBN: 978-93-81345-03-0 (PB)

SAGE Stree Team: Madhuparna Banerjee, Supriya Das, and Neha Sharma

To Badar Begum, who wanted to be an actor,
and my grandmother, Parul Bala,
who loved films.

Bulk Sales

SAGE India offers special discounts
for purchase of books in bulk.
We also make available special imprints
and excerpts from our books on demand.

For orders and enquiries, write to us at

Marketing Department
SAGE Publications India Pvt Ltd
B1/I-1, Mohan Cooperative Industrial Area
Mathura Road, Post Bag 7
New Delhi 110044, India

E-mail us at **marketing@sagepub.in**

Get to know more about SAGE

Be invited to SAGE events, get on our mailing list.
Write today to **marketing@sagepub.in**

This book is also available as an e-book.

CONTENTS

Voices of the Talking Stars

LIST OF ILLUSTRATIONS

(by order of appearance)

FOREWORD

From 2011, the School of Women's Studies, Jadavpur University, began to publish a series of readers for students. There have so far been three titles in four volumes (the first, *Mapping the Field*, is in two volumes). This is the last in the current series. A single volume of essays in Bengali is in the works. We hope that there will be others as new themes emerge and new courses are introduced.

The need for more teaching/learning material in women's studies has been felt for some years. The School of Women's Studies (SWS) teaches an M.Phil course since 2000. The curriculum was revised in 2006 and is currently undergoing another round of revision. By 2006, we had realized some of the difficulties of transacting 'interdisciplinarity' in the classroom. The course draws interested participants from a variety of backgrounds, not only the expected fresh postgraduates from humanities and social sciences, but also students from physics and medicine, psychiatry and biosciences, mature women students returning to the academy with an interest in exploring questions about their own lives and social contexts, NGO workers desiring to learn more about their 'field', and school and college teachers seeking a fresh perspective on their disciplines. At that time, the rather difficult question of finding sufficient teachers was solved by the collective effort of the entire women's studies community in the city. At the present moment, due to the expansion in women's studies undertaken by the University Grants Commission (UGC) during the Eleventh Plan period, the SWS is an advanced centre and has a faculty strength of nearly ten. There can be no doubt that women's studies has entered a new phase of consolidation as an interdisciplinary field and in terms of institutionalization.

The 1990s and early years of the twenty-first century saw a quantum leap in the sheer quantity of literature produced on gender. There was also, more significantly, a major reframing of problems and questions in the field. Yet, the array of existing books and articles are not always available for students and a need was felt to try and bring some of it together in a form easily accessible to students, who may be returning to the academy after some years, or socially disadvantaged students, who found it difficult to collect and collate the material. Around the same time, there was a move in different parts of the country, encouraged by the University Grants Commission to introduce Masters' and even Bachelors' courses in women's studies. Indeed, the subject had been included in the National Eligibility Test (NET) for many years, though there had not been very many takers; the numbers have steeply and steadily risen in the last ten years. Most of the established universities have revised their undergraduate and graduate curricula to introduce 'gender topics' across humanities and social sciences. In some universities, women's studies is an optional course at the undergraduate level. We are occasionally approached by teachers and students for reading material and by undergraduate colleges for help in applying for women's studies centres. The series of Readers was a response to this enormous expansion in teaching and research activities within universities.

We were fortunate that around the same time, the Higher Education Cell of Sir Ratan Tata Trust (Mumbai) at the Centre for the Study of Culture and Society (CSCS, Bangalore) had initiated a grant for building resources in women's studies. Their generous grant gave us the opportunity to mobilize resources for not only teaching our own new courses but also to collaborate with other universities and colleges in their endeavours and, most importantly, undertake the urgent task of producing teaching/learning material. It is with their financial assistance that we have been able to prepare this series of four Readers.

The current volume does not quite fall in the conventional definition of a 'Reader' and yet, we thought, given the expansive scope for interaction between media, film and women's studies, we needed to explore this field. This Reader should be read as an intervention within the scope of film studies as well as an attempt to bring film into an established tradition of 'reading' women's writings within feminist scholarship (a trope we addressed in the third Reader of this series, *Shaping the Discourse: Women's Writings in Bengali Periodicals 1865–1947*). It may be seen as a conceptual and critical intervention, which aims not to merely 'collect' writings by women or on women but to use the lens of gender to understand the gaps within film studies as well as cultural studies, more broadly conceived. It helps us broaden and indeed re-imagine the public sphere, including women's networks, public and memory construction. The writings included in the volume, titled *Voices of the Talking Stars*, are scattered and self-reflexive interviews, essays, biographies and poems by female actors. They explore the complex relationships between cinema, industry, cultures, labour and gender during the studio era (1930–55) and in its immediate aftermath. The editor, Madhuja Mukherjee, envisions these as directed and powerful tools for the writing of film history.

We realize that the potential readership for this series has been envisaged in perhaps rather too generous terms, spanning undergraduate and research students and their teachers. In this our ambition has been shaped by the paucity of textbooks in the Indian market. This statement needs to be qualified somewhat, because our publishers have already published three very successful volumes in the Theorizing Feminism series that focus on concepts and methodology. Mary John's Reader has also been a major contribution in this regard. There have been a few more such series by various publishers, many of them of the highest quality and extremely valuable. Given the rate at which women's studies courses are proliferating, however, we need much more and we need them quickly. We hope this series will serve the purpose of broadening the field. Though at present this series includes four Readers in five volumes (and a Bengali volume of translations from the two-volume *Mapping the Field* is forthcoming), we hope that these will be followed by more in the same vein.

On behalf of the School and for the successful launching of this series of Readers, we must acknowledge many contributions. The members and staff of the School, especially Anindita Bhaduri and Debamitra Talukdar, have greatly helped these efforts. I must thank the Director of the School, Dr. Aishika Chakraborty, for her help in the final stages of the publication of this volume. The staff and faculty of the university are always supportive of the efforts of the School. We thank them all. The university administration too has a hand in this publication. Professor Pradip Narayan Ghosh, Professor Abhijit Chakrabarti, Professor Souvik Bhattacharyya and Dr. Ashish S. Verma, Vice Chancellors, Dr. Pradip Kumar Ghosh, Registrar and G. K. Pattanayak, Finance Officer, played crucial roles in helping us settle administrative difficulties. Stree publications took on the project when it was little more than a plan and we offer them much gratitude. Of course, none of this would have been possible without the generous grant from Sir Ratan Tata Trust. We thank the Trustees for believing in our project and helping us take it forward. At the HE Cell in CSCS Bangalore, we must thank first Tejaswini Niranjana, without whose friendship and intellectual support, there would have been no plan. Rekha Pappu has also been a pillar of support in navigating our way, administratively and intellectually. Ashish Rajadhyaksha has extended his help and co-operation at difficult moments. Sheetal Nandanwar has made the nitty-gritty of administration as easy as she possibly could. To all the members of the HE Cell our sincerest thanks.

We have seen great interest in the previous three titles of the Readers; we hope this volume too will be helpful to teachers and students. Together, if they contribute towards the expansion in the field and draw new enthusiasts amongst our midst, they will have served their purpose well.

May 2015

Samita Sen,
Professor, School of Women's Studies,
Jadavpur University, Kolkata

ACKNOWLEDGEMENTS

During the early stage of my research in film studies, while I frantically examined primary sources on the studio era of Indian cinema with my main focus on New Theatres Ltd., I understood that there lay a plethora of information—articles about female actors, black and white images of stars, gossip columns, fan letters, advertisements of films and film equipments, publicity posters of soaps, cosmetics, medicines, and so on—which could not be included in the dissertation as it required a specialized or dedicated study.

While much of the material eventually became an important section of my Ph.D. thesis, this specific approach that film histories may be problematized through issues of gender grew over the years. As I worked on other areas, found new literature, listened to the magnificent *ghazals* narrated so wistfully by Meena Kumari and interviewed experienced actors, I realized that a certain kind of film history may be *re-written*; furthermore, the important literature produced by Indian Film Studies scholars may also be *re-visited*, if we are able to address and acknowledge the question of gender. It is within such contested terrain that the plan of this project escalated out of proportions and became a book. I am truly grateful to the School of Women's Studies, Jadavpur University, for taking such keen interest in this project, especially Samita Sen for her kind support, Jayeeta Bagchi for sharing the experiences of the making of her own book, Ipshita Chandra for pushing me to take this plunge, Paromita Chakraborty for her encouraging words, Kavita Panjabi for her insightful comments, Madhurima Mukhopadhyay and Atig Ghosh for agreeing to translate certain sections of this project within a very short span of time, as well as the entire staff of the School of Women's Studies, who helped me in very many ways. Moreover, I am indebted to Prakriti Mitra for giving me her personal collections of photographs, some of which have been used in this anthology.

I am particularly grateful to Gulzarji, the eminent writer and director, first, for granting his kind permission to translate Meena Kumari's poems, which he perceptively recovered from her diaries and published as *Tanhaa Chaand*; and second, for the brief conversations I had with him which enriched my understanding of the contexts in which Meena Kumari penned her thoughts. I also wish to thank Moinak Biswas for allowing me to use some of the materials housed in the Media Lab, Department of Film Studies, Jadavpur University; Shubham Roy Chowdhury for being there when one needed a helping hand; my friend and colleague Anindya Sengupta for patiently listening to my entire project. I am thankful to Stree for their enthusiastic responses and incredible support. I am indebted to Samit Sarkar for granting permission to translate sections from Kanan Devi's *Sabare Ami Nomi*. Moreover, I appreciate the encouraging support from my friends and colleagues, especially Subhajit Chatterjee, who has always been there by my side.

I hope that, besides students and scholars of film, media and gender studies, this volume may be useful and enjoyable to a long list of film lovers, including my mother, Manju Mukherjee, who was bitten by the film bug at the young age of seven, and my father, Bibhash Mukherjee, who has always been there as my support system. Finally, I want to specially mention Avik Mukhopadhyay, my confidant and husband, who stood by me through all those nights when I was anxiously trying to finish the first draft of this volume and glean meaning out of a somewhat wide-ranging material. I am deeply grateful to everyone who has collaborated with me in this delightful journey and so happy that I have gained friends in the process.

INTRODUCING VOICES AND VERSES

It may be useful to understand the gendering of film histories by beginning with a close reading of a rather well-known and frequently discussed film like *Charulata* (directed by Satyajit Ray, 1964), though this would mean a deliberate detour, to recognize the larger purpose of this volume. At the outset, I wish to examine three significant sequences from the film to comment on issues of women's writing in India. The film is an adaptation of a short story by Rabindranath Tagore (*Nastaneer*, 1901) and is about a cultured and educated 'lonely wife' (as translated by Ray) who falls in love with her brother-in-law and takes to writing after a series of personal encounters with him.[1] Set in 1879 (and made at the point when Ray was also making films like *Mahanagar*, 1963, which dealt with issues of women's economic freedom), it 'addresses the socio-political movements and the involvement of the *bhadraloks*, the educated middle-class of Bengal'.[2] It is in this context that Bhupati's bored yet sensitive wife, Charulata (aka Charu), finds her world transformed when her friend/brother-in-law Amal storms (back) into her life.[3] Through a series of consecutive scenes, Ray sequentially projects the courses through which Charu gets involved with Amal, and this is imperative for this volume because the 'process' of falling in love is deeply linked with Charu's emergence as a writer and finding her own voice.

Recognized for its magnificent track shots and Subrata Mitra's inventive lighting techniques, as well as Bansi Chandragupta's realistic set design, the film opens by emphasizing how Charu's life is circumscribed by her daily chores, juxtaposing them with shots that suggest her talent in stitching and her keen interest in literature (as she hums 'Bankim, Bankim' and picks a copy of Bankim Chandra Chattopadhyay's novel *Kapalkundala*), music (piano) and the outside world. After Amal's entry into her home, Amal and Charu's discussions on literature (albeit through the initiation of Bhupati, her husband), soon become intense deliberations on contemporary writings and discursive practices of the period, where issues of fiction and non-fiction get intertwined with the women's question. For instance, in the first literary contestation with Amal, while Charu argues for her liking of Bankim Chandra's works, her sister-in-law (Mandar), who is lying on the bed, snores away in oblivious bliss. In the same scene (earlier), Amal reads out from *Prachina ebang Navina*, the influential piece by Bankim Chandra, and asks Mandar if she is the *prachina* ('the erstwhile woman').[4] While Mandar retorts to this by saying that she 'doesn't know', Amal starts a discussion with Charu, the *navina* ('the new woman'), on contemporary writings. This deliberate use of Bankim Chandra's name as well as references to his famous essay and novels, maps the primary concerns of the text.

Such discussions are followed by Amal and Charu's conversations in the garden, which becomes a symbolic domain, a site for nurturing thoughts, where Charu's emotional predicaments are laid bare. Thus, the scenes in the garden are accentuated by Charu's unmindful humming of *'ki jani kishero laagi, prano kore hai, hai...'* ('I don't know what my soul craves for...'). The swing, Charu looking at Amal, the fleeting light on her face and the subtle changes in her mood are obvious indicators reflecting Charu's dilemma. Ray's editing style and sharp cuts further heighten Charu's growing uneasiness and underline the rapid emotional shifts which she undergoes. Gradually, both Charu and Amal appear to motivate each other into writing. While Charu makes beautiful notebooks for Amal and urges him to write ('think and write,' she says) through her constant companionship, for Amal, however, this involvement is somewhat impersonal, as evident in several scenes. Ray repeatedly draws our attention to the physical act of writing through various details and uses of close-up shots.

A shot-by-shot analysis (of the second scene in the garden) shows how the erotic and the phatic are intricately linked. For instance, *a*) sitting on the swing, Charu hums 'thank you'; *b*) shots of the foliage (Charu's point of view shot) followed by the camera tilting up to a mother and child; *c*) Charu's disheartened expression; *d*) cut to Amal's face (Charu's point of view), *e*) close-up on Charu, she smiles unmindfully and then appears worried. Thereafter, she quickly recovers from this intimate moment as soon as she hears Amal's voice. It is after this sequence that through personal humiliation, Charu starts writing. However, if one reads the visual signs carefully (including the fact that Amal holds a flute throughout his conversations with Charu, at the point he urges her to write about her village fair), it is evident that Charu's literary drive is deeply erotic in nature and her initiation into writing happens through her initiation into love. Ray, working within the larger notion of national–modern, uses a contemporary language (for dialogues) and tone, which along with the performances of the actors, underline the relevance of the subject even at the point the film was being made.[5]

In a later sequence, after Amal has sent his article to an established journal, Charu appears evidently dejected to know about the public circulation of his essays (which she had imagined to be her personal possession). Like other occasions, she hides her feelings and appears to be busy with household errands. The hierarchy in the realm of writing

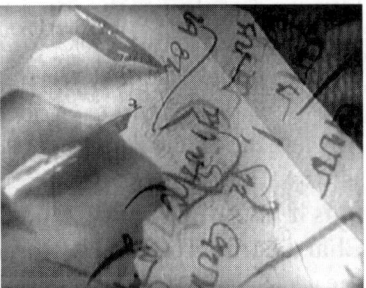

Charu's straightforward style; Amal's stylized handwriting

becomes apparent as Bhupati enters the scene. Armed with his political journal *The Sentinel*, Bhupati first ridicules Amal's aesthetic (and political) concerns, then goes to their bedroom and engages in a political dialogue with Charu.[6] A distraught Charu waits anxiously with a broom in her hand. Bhupati requests her to smell his paper. Later, in the same sequence, while Amal (in a caustic tone) tells Charu that he now deserves the respect of an author, what becomes perceptible is the contested field within which Charu or women begin to write. What may seem like a personal issue or a romantic scuffle emerges as a significant link with larger political topics of women's writing in India. Moinak Biswas (1999: 10) explains:

> Bhupati writes politics and in English, Amal and Charu create literature in Bangla. And then a further division, Amal writes for public circulation, in an ornate register overlaid with conventions of style ['*Amabashyar Chand*' for instance]; Charu would write for a strictly private exchange, in an unadorned style through which she can 'write herself' into the literary discourse. Towards the end,... [she] plan[s] a poignantly illusory reconciliation between the poles of the masculine and feminine, the home and the world, the political and the affective... .[7]

The complexities of the plot emerge as Charu's thoughts grow beyond the 'private exchange', and out of rage, despair, love and jealousy she begins to write, and 'write herself' into public discourses. One of the major conjectures of this volume, in fact, is to understand the significance of emotion, affection, desire and the processes through which such issues frame women's writing. While Charu begins with somewhat sentimental expressions like, 'The Cuckoo's Cry', she later puts it as 'The Cuckoo's Pain'. Seated in the same swing, later, Charu contemplates and remembers the river in her village, the *melas* (fairs) and the people. The psychedelic montage of faces highlights an idiom, which Amal, later (while admitting

his own 'stupidity'), describes as effortless and spontaneous. Ray juxtaposes the stylized handwriting of Amal with
the simple, straightforward writing of Charu.[8] Nevertheless,
soon after her article is published in *Bisvabandhu* (Ray supposedly refers to the reputed journal *Bangadarshan* here),
Charu rolls up a copy of the journal, runs towards Amal, hits
him vigorously, then runs out erratically to get *pan* (beetle
leaf) and eventually bursts into tears as she embraces Amal
passionately. Such emotional outbursts, which remain con-
spicuously ambiguous to Amal until the very end, insistently
underline the larger history of transformations where navina
and prachina (or Charu and Mandar) address their own
dilcmmas, just as they are pitted against each other at this
historical magic hour.[9] Charu's pose (hands on her waist),
and her expressions (that of pure vengeance), as well as her
cries, '*Dekho, dekho, dekho* ...' ('Just look') as she hits Amal on
his head with the journal, in actuality show the meaningful
connections between desire and writing. Unmistakably, Amal
is dumbfounded in a situation like this. Despite her resolution not to write again, Charu in reality takes the journal
with her indicating such possibilities in future. As a matter
of fact, it is through a series of suffering that Charu eventually (towards the end) accepts her identity as a writer, and
encourages Bhupati to revive his journal, suggesting that she
could co-edit the journal, which would have separate sections
on social issues (in Bengali) and politics (in English).

Even in moments, which are darkly and intensely bound
by deep longing, Charu and Amal engage in a game of allit-
eration, just as they play with the alphabet 'B'.[10] Here, it is
Charu who prompts the game in a subtle way. She says, 'You
will first go to Burdwan [in Bengal], then to Britain.' Amal
catches up slowly, and then responds by describing his plans.

Amal: 'No, first Burdwan, then *biye* [marriage], and then
Britain.'
Charu (cuts in): 'And then?'

Amal: 'After that, Bristol.'

Charu (anxiously): 'And then…? Barrister? After that?'

Amal: 'Thereafter, Black-native, Back to Bengal….'

Charu (with disappointment): 'Bengal? *Byas?*' [That's it?]

Amal: 'And, Bankim. Babu Bankim Chandra. Byron to Bankim… *Bishabriksha*….'[11]

Charu: And, *Bouthan*…?[12]

While, on the one hand Charu's expression ('byas') reveals her emotional expectations from Amal, on the other, at the same point in time, she seems to enquire, 'That's it? The game is over, already?' The persistence in playing with (the meaning of) words, names of authors, the language and its cultural implications as well as the very act of writing, along with the woman's role in it, become crucial in this context.

Partha Chatterjee's pathbreaking book *The Nation and Its Fragments: Colonial and Postcolonial Histories* brought up two significant aspects pertaining to issues of gender.[13] In the chapter 'The Nation and Its Women', Chatterjee discusses in the essay, the paradox of the women's question (throughout the nineteenth century), by locating it within the framework of modernization. He shows how cultural reformers were selective about the ways in which they adapted the liberal worldview from Europe. It is in this situation that the problem of 'new woman' arises. Chatterjee explains that while the outer world (*bahir*) was dominated by the Europeans, for the colonized people it was fundamental to produce an imagined sovereignty within the inner world (*ghar*).[14] He writes:

> [a]pplying the inner/outer distinction to the matter of concrete day-to-day living separates the social space into ghar and bahir, the home and the world. The world is the external, domain of the material; the home represents one's inner spiritual self, one's true identity. The world…is also typically the domain of the male. The home in its essence must remain unaffected by the profane activities of the material world—and woman is its representation.[15]

Voices of the Talking Stars

Several scholars have contested such dichotomies between spiritual/material, ghar/bahir and feminine/masculine. New writings, however, have proven that attempts to study political-cultural spheres as neatly divided or as 'concrete' domains within the everyday are problematic.[16]

Nevertheless, the question of education vis-à-vis the new woman is a pertinent one. Chatterjee shows how by producing 'textbooks, periodicals, and creative works' in the mother tongue, the *bhadromahila* was trained to become a refined and cultured woman.[17] Curiously, in *Charulata*, in the scenes set in the garden, Charu fervidly reacts to Amal saying, 'If you don't write, I shall become answerable to brother.... Brother will think that I am not teaching you anything.' Charu retorts, 'Why, because he said so...?' Amal cuts in by saying, 'He has not stated that if you take the responsibility of my wife's education I shall pay you.' Charu retorts to this by leaving the place abruptly. And, it is not until Charu publishes her work that this rift is mended.

Such narratives, as a matter of fact, complicate issues of women's education, because on the one hand Charu in due course writes what Amal had suggested, but on the other hand, she self-consciously opposes such suggestions and Amal's approach in order to find her own style. Chatterjee discusses how Charulata, the heroine in Rabindranath Tagore's story,

> ...first tried her hand at writing, she began with an essay called 'The August Cloud' but soon discovered that it read too much like another essay called 'The July Moon' written by her brother-in-law Amal. She then proceeded to write about the Kali temple in the village in which she had lived as a child...[18]

Her style (as described by Tagore), had a 'simplicity and charm of its own', with the 'richness of rural idiom'. While Ray tried to capture this 'simplicity' through his visuals, the purpose of this volume is not merely to examine such 'simple' styles and the content of women's writing, but to study thoroughly the varied modes and concerns projected by women writers. It hopes to locate as well these writings within larger histories, forms and cultures of literature and poetry. However, this volume does not merely aspire to contest certain theoretical frameworks. The aim is to bring together a range of literature that helps to revisit our disciplinary conjectures and histories. Additionally, the objective here is not to add to the existing literature either on cinema or on women's writings. The intention is to use gender as a critical device to understand the conditions overlooked so far.

For instance, Chatterjee writes at length about Rasasundari Devi's writings as well as Nati Binodini and others to show how women's narratives were rarely given the status of *charit* (or biographies). He writes, the 'most common name by which they [women's writing] were described was *smrtikatha*: "memoirs" or more accurately, "stories from memory"'.[19] Preceding his work, Susie Tharu and K. Lalita had edited a landmark collection (in two volumes) and brought together, through an interventionist approach, a range of material (written in different languages in India), lost and found through the centuries.[20] In the introduction to the first volume, Tharu and Lalita observed:

> [a]t one level the two volumes of *Women Writing in India* are a joyous retrieval of artifacts that signify women's achievement. At another, they represent a difficult and inventive moment in the theory and practice of feminist criticism.[21]

The purpose of these volumes, as described by Tharu and Lalita, was to create a room for 'conceptual and critical' interventions.[22] In a similar vein, the purpose here is *not to bring together* what female actors have written, but to *edit* a volume that helps us to understand the gaps within our own disciplines (both within film studies as well as methods of writing political-cultural history). To use Christine Gledhill's words, 'broadening the conception of the public sphere, it [such investigation] opens up the social history of cinema as it circulates through women's networks, both public and memory construction.'[23] This, however, is not to suggest that all the writings chosen here are by self-conscious 'feminist' authors. The scattered and self-reflexive interviews, essays, biographies and poems by female actors, nevertheless, show the complex relationships between cinema, industry, cultures, labour and gender during the studio era (1930–55) and the few years immediately after its collapse. In my opinion, these voices and verses can be more pointed and powerful tools to examine an intermittent film history. I have primarily used writings by 'actors', including that of Mae West (Hollywood's foremost actor and writer, also popular in Bengal and else-where) to explore how they might have 'acted upon' the situation when the film industry was forming. Moreover, the material by itself is remarkably important and brings to light information regarding the studio structures in the 1930s, as well as the rare papers (especially the letters by the little known actor Ratan Bai) found through research show the complex field of industrial networks and the overlap of dispa-rate areas of performances. In a complicated way, a number of these writings emphasize on the relationship between labour, gender and desire.[24]

By and large, female actors have been either seen as beautiful images in popular journalist writings or the lives of female stars have been used as a useful device to analyse the intricacy of the industry and the reception of films.[25] The purpose of choosing a particular timeframe—the studio era and beyond—therefore, is to facilitate us to recognize the role of women and their views at the juncture when the economy of cinema was being institutionalized. I have included writings, which in principle connect questions of gender, sexuality and work with cinema. By definition, I have excluded a host of other articles, which describe the lives of popular actors, or their achievements, and so on. Larger issues of the film industry became a significant marker as I sought for articles, interviews, letters and essays written by female actors. The technique and skill of these women writers who were confronting a masculine domain also became important for me.

While within the scope of film studies and feminist interventions, Ann Kaplan's edited volume, Molly Haskell's and Mary Ann Doane's writings, Jennifer M. Bean and Diane Negra's edited collection, along with Judith Butler's challenging theorizations and Laura Mulvey's outstanding essay remain landmark works, Jackie Stacey's research on female spectators and the paradoxes of consumption, as well as Lant and Periz's more recent empirical research bring up the subject of reception of popular films by women.[26] In the *Red Velvet Seat*, Lant and Periz have brought together several writings to comment on the enormously knotty ways in which women receive cinema. Sections like 'Why We Go to the Movies' and 'Cinema as Job' are important within this framework. Moreover, Vicki Callahan's recent volume interrogates feminist film history, to produce a feminist film historiography, which

Chitrapanji *(Bengali): one of the popular journals of the 1930s*

is grounded on empirical considerations. Her section on 'Excavating Early Cinema' is also crucial in this context.[27]

While considering a larger background of feminist historiography for films, this compilation grows from an extensive research conducted on the studio era of Indian cinemas. Beginning with a fellowship from the National Film Archive of India in 1998, until more recently working on a project under the UGC Minor Research scheme (2006–2008), I have been meticulously examining popular journals of the 'Talkie' period. The study includes scanning of rather obscure, scattered and somewhat randomly found material in periodicals like *Batayan* (Bengali), *Bioscope* (Bengali), *Chitralekha* (Bengali), *Chitrapanji* (Bengali), *Chitrapat* (Hindi), *Cinema Sansar* (Hindi), *Dipali* (Bengali), *Filmfare, Film India, Film Land, Film World, Kheyali* (Bengali), *Nachghar* (Bengali), *New Cinema Sansar* (Hindi), *Rangbhoomi* (Hindi), *Sight and Sound, Talk-A-Tone and Varieties Weekly.* Much of this work has been conducted at the National Film Archive of India, Pune; British Film Institute, London; Bangiya Sahitya Parishad, National Library, Kolkata, as well as some lesser-known film archives located in suburban Kolkata. Articles from both *Chitrapanji* and *Dipali* located through the work at the Media Lab (a NRTT, Mumbai, and Jadavpur University project) have also been helpful.

While the focus of my earlier research including my Ph.D. dissertation has been the film industry, the economy of technologies and culture, and the history of film companies (particularly that of New Theatres Ltd.), the present study brings up material that may be referred to as 'marginal notes' found irregularly in the periodicals. Furthermore, the frame of study have been extended both in terms of time (up to 1970s) and space (up to Hollywood, its stars and Indian fans) in order to first, include influential writings by female actors, and second, to include aspects like desire and disquiet as new categories of analysis. Moreover, such material also highlights the fact that cinema in the subcontinent did not grow in some pre-modern backyard. While articles (written by men) on female stars, their careers and personal lives, and so on, connected to issues of morality and sexuality are rampant, there are rather few articles where female actors actually voice their own experiences. Hence, while the illusive face of the female star is a regular feature of such journals, the most common topic is the 'conduct' of these female actors, which are associated with larger questions of romance, sexuality, body, masculinity, and so on.

It is in this context that this volume brings together somewhat rare writings by female actors (written between the late 1920s and 1970s), which comment on the film industry and broader social issues. The purpose, as mentioned earlier, is not merely to showcase women's writings on cinema; it is through such articles that one hopes to examine the existing frameworks of film history, culture and politics, which are so intrinsically involved with problems of gender. I have also chosen the interviews of entrepreneurs as well as members of the Board of Censor, who were interviewed at the point when the Indian Cinematograph Committee Report was being prepared (during 1927–28), as decisive aspects of Indian cinema.

WRITING AND ARCHIVING THE SELF

In connection to the present work, I particularly wish to mention three influential autobiographies written by female actors. The autobiography of Bhanumathi Ramakrishna, titled *Musings* is a case in point.[28] Paluvayi Bhanumathi Ramakrishna joined the film industry in 1935 and was an actor, director, singer, music composer, as well as a poet and a writer.[29] The Andhra Pradesh Sahitya Academy awarded her the best short storywriter award for her popular short stories *Attagari Kathalu*. Similarly, Mrs. Durga Khote, a leading actor of the period who started her career with Marathi films, was also the first female actor to start a film company in the region. She had also made documentary films. In the foreword to the book, Gayatri Chatterjee writes about the 'Contours' of her 'Life and Work' and states:

> [a] man and a woman are situated together at any time in contemporary history, but she does not share in that equally with a man—their histories are always different. Not many women in the modern period could reap the benefits of modernity as men did; for those women who did, modernity did not come to them in equal terms. In fact, what we see is how women often write in spite of all odds and obstacles. And even they themselves construct their selves differently.[30]

While Durga Khote's 'regal' presence (that dwarfed the men around her) remains a powerful image within film cultures, she indeed was (as advertised forcefully) one of the first women from a 'respectable' family to join cinema. Her narrative, *I, Durga Khote*, besides showing the ups and downs of her personal life, throws light on the production of early talkies like *Maya Machhindra* (1932) and the functioning of the film industry. About the New Theatres Ltd., she writes:

> Mr. Birendra Nath Sircar, the owner of New Theatres, ...had stepped into the film industry with high hopes, thinking of it as artistic business. But unfortunately he failed financially .... New Theatres suffered losses because its directors formed cliques. Finally, the company went into financial decline.[31]

Undoubtedly, certain points she makes here are her own perceptions, nevertheless, it also reinstates the fact that in the thirties the studios operated through the logics of kinship and were totally at a loss when the industrial structure changed in the context of the Second World War.[32] She writes:

> [d]uring 1934 and 1935, I acted in four films that were made in Calcutta. I signed a four-month contract for each

one of them and was paid Rs 2500 per month. At the end of every shooting schedule, I would return to Bombay. I earned Rs 40,000 during that period.[33]

This statement becomes crucial as we contextualize it and locate it within the larger spectrum of economy and politics. For instance, after the First World War when foreign trade decreased, the domestic market became accessible. Besides the growth of cotton and jute mills in the twenties (in Calcutta, Bombay, and so on), alternate trade like telecommunications became a rewarding option in the thirties. While some work has been done on private investments not much study has been done to consider cinema in India as an industry and examine either the growth of independent studios in the twenties or big-scale organized systems in the thirties.[34] Indeed, the Wall Street Crash (1929) brought about a sudden fall in the prices of agricultural products and created a disorder in the export-oriented colonial economy. By 1935–36, the British strove to develop the textile industry and non-traditional items like electrical goods, telecommunication-wireless apparatus and sugar machinery, which were almost equal in value to the textiles exported by the British to India. In fact, in 1936, the *Journal of Motion Picture Society of India* claimed that cinema together with its associate industries (like the printing press) had a turnover and a labour force that was much bigger than other large-scale industries (like the cement industry). In this context, if we are to compare the salaries of Durga Khote or Sulochana (Ruby Myers) during this period and use them as evidences of the industrial conditions, then these become important facts through which we may comprehend the alternative structure of the Indian economy.

It is within this structure that I chose to edit and translate Kanan Devi's autobiography, *Sabare Ami Nomi* (co-authored by Sandhya Sen) from Bengali.[35] Kananbala, née Devi, was a popular actor-singer of the thirties. She acted in both Bengali and Hindi films. *Mukti* (Dir. P.C. Barua, 1937), *Vidyapati*

(Dir. Debaki Bose, 1938) and *Street Singer* (Dir. Phani Mazumdar, 1938) are some of her most popular films.[36] Her outstanding performance in *Vidyapati* where she played the medieval poet's companion was diametrically different from the role of bhadromahila she played in *Mukti*. During this period she was constantly competing with stars like Devika Rani, and letters from her fans as well as editorial responses in journals like *Film India* are testimonies of the fact. As a matter of fact, poems written about her (by the fans) reflect a significant aspect of the popular cultures of the period.[37] Kanan Devi set up Shrimati Pictures in 1949 and produced films later in her career. In her autobiography she writes about the ups and downs of her career, as well as the instances when she received awards and recognition.[38] Moreover, she writes in detail about the day-to-day activities of the studios, the rehearsals, the role of the stars, co-actors, directors, music composers, musical compositions, and so on. Kanan Devi's somewhat languid style has been retained here to understand *how* women write when they pen their memoirs and the ways in which these may *re-frame* a history, which was effectively beyond them. I have particularly chosen the section on New Theatres for two reasons. First, it connects with my own interest in the history of institutions and studios. Second, through another letter (cited in this volume), written by a lesser-known actor named Ratan Bai, who engages in a dialogue with New Theatres, the image of New Theatres as a 'respectable' production house is somewhat disturbed and scathing details of the functioning of the film industry are revealed. For instance, New Theatres' publicity officer had written the following open letter:

> ...it seems rather contradictory for Miss Ratan Bai to complain of our Managing Director seeking to ruin her reputation as a star, when it was New Theatres who picked her up as Miss Imambandi of 216, Bow Bazar Street and made of her Miss Ratan Bai of 'All-India' fame.[39]

In the consecutive letter, Ratan Bai not only accepts her own background nonchalantly, she also reclaims her position as a talented performer and singer. Ratan Bai writes:

> Mr. Sircar has laid much stress on the point that I have been picked upon from Bowbazar Street before which I was a nonentity and from Imambandi they have made me Ratan Bai of all-India fame. Did I ever approached [sic] the officials of New Theatres Ltd, to give me a job or they approached me to join their company? ...May I enquire, whether they 'picked up' or not hundreds of persons from Sonagachi, Rambagan, Harkata Gully, Bowbazar etc., and how many of them have acquired all-India fame? [the extract represented here appears as in the original.][40]

New Theatres Ltd., established in 1931, Kolkata, indeed was one of the most influential production houses in Bengal.[41] Making films in both Bengali and Hindi, its persuasive power emerged out of its well-structured production-distribution-exhibition system, as well as through the kinds of films they popularized. Ever since its inception, New Theatres and its proprietor, Birendra Nath Sircar, have remained one of the most significant emblems of the studio era of Indian cinema.[42] In fact, as Madan Theatres' economic control weakened in the early thirties, studios launched by Bengali entrepreneurs appeared like a resurgence of Bengali self-worth and sub-nationalism.[43] For instance, when Sircar engineered New Theatres and instituted a certain ('literally') cinematic tendency in Bengal, more or less all stalwarts of cinema, theatre, literature and music industries joined the company. Moreover, when Arya Film Co., with which Sircar was initially associated made its first film *Buker Bojha*, it generated great expectations. *Bioscope* (1930) wrote: 'We thought since the company comprises of educated youth at least their films would do us proud....'

Eminent directors, musicians, technicians, authors, theatre personalities like Nitin Bose, Mukul Bose, Rai Chand Boral,

Pankaj Mullick, Timir Baran Bhattacharya, K. C. Dey, Sisir Kr. Bhaduri, Premankur Atorthy, Sailajananda Mukhopadhyay and others joined the studio. Even noble laureate Rabindranath Tagore's only cinematic venture, *Natir Puja* (1932), took place under New Theatres' patronage just as the popular author Sarat Chandra Chattopadhyay sold the rights of almost all his novels to the house. *Chandidas* (Bengali, 1932), *Puran Bhakt* (Hindi, 1933), *Meerabai/Rajrani Meera* (Bengali/Hindi, 1933), *Devdas* (Bengali/Hindi, 1935), *President* (Hindi, 1936), *Mukti* (Bengali/Hindi, 1937), *Vidyapati* (Bengali/Hindi, 1938), *Dharti Mata* (Hindi, 1938), *Street Singer* (Hindi, 1938), *Wapas* (Hindi, 1943), *Udayer Pathey* (Bengali 1944) are few of the most successful films of New Theatres.

New Theatres intended to produce a particular kind of cinema that may be described as 'purposeful'.[44] However, the filmography, reviews, letters to the editors, photographs and other publicity data indicate that New Theatres produced a highly heterogeneous body of films. A thorough reading of these extra-cinematic texts may lead one to understand the broader cultural politics in Bengal. The overall 'politics of culture' at this point in time not only produced a host of writings but also a great number of divergent films that truly examine the established cultural history of the era. A closer reading shows several ruptures within the bhadralok projects, products and 'pantheons' of culture. Through New Theatres' history and a close reading of the ways in which its history has been written, one may re-read issues of the national–modern, and the problems of identity politics in Bengal.

While a group of remarkably successful people moved to the studio for economic stability, New Theatres produced a cultural sphere where even stalwarts like Tagore experimented with this new idiom. As Rani Burra suggests, 'New Theatres was known for its "elitist" style, its aestheticism and its "cultured" self-consciousness. Their films often had to face empty front benches and packed balconies.'[45] With its commencement, New Theatres instituted a certain kind of film culture through the adaptation of Sarat Chandra Chattopadhyay's popular novels to cinema. It constituted (by exploring the interiority of the characters as well as through the uses of complicated dialogue styles) spatial specificities (of cities and villages) and character prototypes. As mentioned earlier, New Theatres intended to produce 'purposeful' cinema. Its self-conscious 'cultured' aesthetics became a characteristic feature as they portrayed themselves as the 'cathedral of culture' and often quoted Goethe, Voltaire in their publicity flyers. While the Madan Theatres, despite their international network as well as their 'rights' to adapt Bankim Chandra Chattopadhyay's novels to films, were often criticized for 'infusing Parsee tastes' and 'cheap thrills and foreign ethos' to Bengali sophistication and cinema, their economic triumph was seen as a point of distress, and many popular journals urged the *Bangali* to rise to the cause.[46] It is important to note how bhadralok objectives converged at the New Theatres, as it not only became a 'symbol' of economic triumph but also an institution of/for/by the bhadralok, where economic achievements were often displaced onto the site of culture and at times vice-versa.

In reality, very few producers have gained as much respect as Sircar. Much of it grew out from his social positioning, reputation and in the ways in which he engineered a cultural 'movement' of sorts. His speech titled 'Film–Its Place in National Life', at a film seminar in 1955 locates the objectives of New Theatres' bastion. Sircar asserted:

> The pressure of modern society leaves little leisure to the millions to lead a full life. To these the film, two hours a week, re-creates through music, dance and drama, the visions which lie buried deep in their subconscious, being themselves the inheritors of the cultural heritage of the glorious Bharat that was. Should not we, the filmmakers, then rise equal to our opportunities to recreate the vision of our cultural past and cast them in a new mould to inspire our present? [47]

This lengthy discussion on New Theatres becomes a crucial grounding to understand what a little known actor (especially in contemporary times) like Ratan Bai was in actuality contesting. Her letters (written in English) addressed to New Theatres, illustrate her own position and her credibility as an actor, as well as the various routes through which actors joined the studios.[48] Indeed, Ratan Bai, who has been somewhat ignored both by New Theatres as well as by film historians, was in reality the star of *Yahoodi Ki Ladki* (Dir. Aga Hashar, 1933). Virchand Dharamsey writes in 'Advent of Sound in Indian Cinema: Theatre, Orientalism, Action, and Magic':

> New Theatres productions *Josh-e-Mohabbat* (1932) and *Zinda Lash* (1932,) [*sic*] Aga Hashar's *Yahoodi Ki Ladki* (1933) and *Karwan-e-Hyat* (1935) directed by Premankur Atorthy were all Oriental films. Nanubhai Vakil made *Yahoodi Ki Beti* (Desai films, 1956) that brought back the memories of *Yahoodi Ki Ladki*. S.D. Narang also remade it in 1957 as did Bimal Roy under the title *Yahoodi* in 1958.[49]

Certainly, if three different directors were reworking *Yahoodi Ki Ladki* in three consecutive years, the plot must have had a certain significance in the history of popular cinemas. Therefore, when Ratan Bai (of *Yahoodi Ki Ladki* fame) enquires about her role or absence of it in *Karwan-e-Hyat*, it does throw light on the studio structures and its prejudices. My personal conversations with Jamuna Barua, in addition, also uncover such details and issues of gender biases.

For instance, Jamuna Barua emerged as a shining star or as the Paro of *Devdas* in 1935, though she had a somewhat shrouded past and a more mystifying present. Apparently she came from Lucknow (although in the personal conversation conducted about a decade earlier, she insisted that she came from Assam, which is basically Pramathesh Chandra Barua's native place), and was made into a star overnight by the enigmatic actor-director P. C. Barua. What emerged from my conservations with Jamuna Barua is an alternative picture of the artist (or of Barua), who was somewhat responsible in making her into 'a cloud-clapped star' of sorts. Yet, her deep love and admiration for Barua's work, along with Barua's own predicaments (as projected in his films like *Devdas, Mukti, Adhikar* 1939), in actuality narrate a very complex story of the emergent modernity in India, and the navina-prachina dichotomy. Moreover, Jamuna Barua's memories vis-à-vis the making of *Devdas*, along with Kananbala's detailed descriptions of the shooting of *Mukti, Sathi* (also *Street Singer* in Hindi; Dir. Phani Mazumdar, 1938) and *Sapure* (Dir. Debaki Bose, 1939) are crucial in understanding the production procedure within the studios. Curiously, both Jamuna Barua and Kananbala insist that they never had any opportunity to speak to B. N. Sircar, the proprietor of New Theatres. Therefore, the style of the letters addressed to and written by Ratan Bai of '216 Bow Bazar Street' is intriguing. Ratan Bai, in no uncertain terms, describes how they were picked up from 'Bow Bazar' (red light area) and elsewhere, and throws light on the larger oversights of film historiography and draws attention to the materiality of history. Especially in the case of the history of New Theatres, which has been imagined as a bastion of the bhadralok and has been studied as a house comprising primarily bhadraloks, as well, repeatedly described as a company making only 'literary' films, such archival material underline the difficulties of history writing and re-invent a more complicated history of cinema and culture.[50] It also shows the multiple layers and sub-texts of our social-cultural everyday, and that history of cinema cannot be studied with the certainty of uncomplicated, independent and uninterrupted facts.

THE PROBLEM OF RESPECTABLE LADIES

The focus of this section is to examine the functioning of the film industry through issues of gender and work. In connection to this, a section from Samik Bandopadhyay's work (1993) ('Stars Speak') on the writings of actors like Sulochana/Ruby Myers, Chandravati Devi and others becomes a significant reference.[51] This section tackles the extremely interesting debate on whether 'respectable ladies' should or should not join cinema. For instance, an anonymous lady artiste writes:

> Before joining the films, I too had thought it would be an honest means of livelihood. The world is not aware as regards the inner life of the studios in Bengal.... The actresses that are usually found to support a film career come from houses of ill fame.... Under the prevailing conditions [where 'the producing companies here are formed...to satisfy their lust and passion', etc.] it is my candid opinion that my sisters, educated and cultured as they are, should not be lured by high-sounding promises of helping out of the present unemployment problem. It is not advisable for any society girl to join films....[52]

While the candidness of her tone is undeniable, such moralistic overtones produced a series of articles and fervent debates in *Filmland*. This volume includes a rejoinder by Sabita Devi in order to explore subjects of respectability, which was one of the primary concerns of the early period.[53] Surely, large sections of the popular press insistently dealt with the topic of 'respectability' of the female actors, their background and present life styles, as well as questions of their everyday activities, marriage, chastity and various other moral issues pertaining to their personal lives. For instance, *Chitrapanji*, published a series of articles which bring up subjects like 'Vulgarity in Films', 'The Trap of Cinema', 'Women in Films', 'Actresses', and so on.[54] Similarly, the *Puja* special of the same periodical in the same year, brought out articles like 'Film and Sex'; other articles like 'Should Women Dance or Not?' as well as those that mentioned the Censor Board, educational films, and so on were further published.[55]

Comparisons with Hollywood stars, their charm, skilfulness, style and lives were also a common feature of the period.[56] In fact, Indian filmmakers, writers and the audiences in general were regularly exposed to American films, as well as European films.[57] A few magazines from Bengal like *Filmland* and *Chitrapanji* consistently published photographs of such films and stars, along with articles on their lives, films, gossips and so on. Briefly, it must be noted that during the colonial period, the audiences in India, especially in Calcutta (and Bombay), did not reside in cultural solitude.[58] Instead, the frequent releases on American films created a vibrant fan culture and a milieu for discursive practices. Fan writings, moreover, were a strong and notable tendency. For instance, Nabakumar Mukhopadhyay wrote a poem about Greta Garbo, describing how 'Garbo kisses him in his dreams' and the manner in which he 'experiences heavenly bliss on earth'.[59] Likewise, Girija Kumar Basu in his poem '*Sukh-Dukkho*'[60] pens a critique of Greta Garbo's films, appreciates the thespian Sisir Kumar Bhaduri and praises Sadhana Bose and her landmark film *Alibaba* (Dir. Madhu Bose, 1937). Indeed, such comparisons were common, as reflected in Bibhudan Roychowdhury's poems on the 'magical world of Hollywood'.[61] Similarly, Raghunath Kundu in 'Our Trio' describes the appeal of actresses and elaborates the ways in which Kananbala seemingly 'gleans the nectar of spring (flowers)'.[62] In fact, Kananbala's sweet voice was a momentous reason for her massive popularity and was highlighted in particular sequences of *Shesh Uttar* (Dir. P. C. Barua, 1942). A number of these poems written by male fans repeatedly used expressions like '*maya*' (illusion), '*chhaya*' (image or literally shadow, another word for cinema) and '*kaya*' (the body or face of the star). While it was common to picture the film star as the beloved, Ramnarayan Das's poem also ridiculed such fanfare and wrote how such an imaginary beloved was a peculiar mix of Kananbala's smile,

Joan Crawford's eyes, Sabita Devi's nose, Zubeida's long hair, Mary Pickford's lips, and so on.[63]

Thus, while it may appear somewhat tricky that this book includes a translation from Bengali of Mae West as well as a discussion on her marvellous screenplay, such writings provoke rather dense arguments on gender and morality, and *work as a tool* that can interrogate more immediate problems.[64] Mae West's article and many such essays (translated in Bengali and published for the Bengali readers) also highlight the fact that Indian cinema did not grow in a third world ghetto of sorts. Instead, its makers as well as the viewers were rather well conversant with films made in Soviet Russia, Germany, France, America and England. While in the article translated here she mentions that she has written it for her fans, Mae West, however states:

> People attack me viciously because I portray sex forthrightly on screen. If I had represented it through a veil of literary conceit and mystification, perhaps, it would have come across as less terrifying. This is something I completely fail to understand—because sex is not necessarily vulgar. I don't think it is anymore so than eating. Sex is never vulgar except to vulgar people ... .
>
> *If you are interested to know about my private life, then I can tell you this—I'm no angel. Who's going to carry the weight of wings? But, I'm happy and you could compare my daily life to the standard lifestyle of any woman. I do not drink or smoke. I do not like the taste of alcohol; so, I do not drink.* [italics as in the original][65]

Besides the fact that Mae West wrote the screenplay of *I'm No Angel* (1933), which have been referred to in this volume, her caustic tone, along with her 'quotable quotes' show that when women write they do not necessarily apply a simple style nor do they deal with uncomplicated issues. For instance, Mae West retorts, 'I believe in censorship. I made a fortune out of it', or 'I didn't discover curves; I only uncovered them'. Similarly, she said, 'I enjoyed the courtroom as just another stage but not so amusing as Broadway',[66] and 'I generally avoid temptation unless I can't resist it'. And, some of the more famous lines are: 'I wrote the story myself. It's all about a girl who lost her reputation but never missed it', and 'When I'm good, I'm very good. When I'm bad, I'm better'.[67]

Mae West's double meaning humorous lines become further meaningful when we study her journey from Broadway to the cinemas. She was a comedian, a playwright and a screenwriter. Her first role in the Broadway play, *Sex*, was also written, directed and produced by her. While critics disliked the show, the play was a success. The infamous show, however, was stopped; the theatre was raided, resulting in West's arrest along with the rest of the cast. She was prosecuted on morals' charges and on 19 April 1927, she was sentenced to ten days of jail. Her popularity, nevertheless, enhanced. Soon, she also proposed a play (*Drag*) on homosexuality. In 1932, at the age of thirty-eight (which was a secret), West was offered a contract by Paramount Pictures.[68] She made her film debut with *Night after Night*. In *Night after Night* in the first scene, while a girl exclaims, 'Goodness, what beautiful diamonds!' West replies, 'Goodness had nothing to do with it, dearie'. Her straight forward, sharp wit and her throaty voice used in *Night after Night* was followed up in *She Done Him Wrong* and *I'm No Angel* in 1933. While *She Done Him Wrong* was a big success and was nominated for the Academy Awards, it apparently saved Paramount from bankruptcy; the film, moreover, also introduced the legendary

Mae West in a scene from I'm No Angel

star Cary Grant. In 1959, West published her autobiography, *Goodness Had Nothing to Do with It*.[69]

Indeed, to use Mae West's lines differently, it's not the women in cinema that count, but the cinema or the history of cinema in these women.[70] Her life was an open book, as it were, through which one many read the ways in which women writers contributed to narrative cinema and used femininity as thereby redefining popular modes of address. For instance, while the sharp Hollywood wit and one-liners become part of its popular approach, there is little doubt that these carry a masculine overture. In this context, West's interventions, or her utterances, produce its own resonances. It seems to use its specific mode of expression and subvert the structure from within. This volume includes such writings by women, which were circulated within the public domain, and had recast the narratives of cinema and disrupted bhadralok conjectures. For instance, the *Puja* issue of *Dipali* (1936) includes advertisements of day and night ('Otin') cream and perfumed oil for 'contemporary women', along with advertisements for skin ointments, ghee, Darjeeling tea, child care products, radio sets, Megaphone records (and recorded plays), cooking ware, soaps, syrups, sweets, innerwear, homeopathy medicines, shops for sex talk, contraceptive devices, manuals on how to kiss, birth control pills, Swiss Viagra, breast enhancement

Advertisement for Dipali, *a popular journal during the 1930s*

creams (namely, 'Bustofine'), shoes (like Bata as well as nationalist 'charkha' chappals/slippers), ammunitions, life insurance, camera, lens, and so on. This particular issue of *Dipali* also included translations of haikus by eminent authors like Radharani Devi (mother of writer Nabaneeta Dev Sen, who is also remembered as one of the few upper-caste radical women who re-married during 1930s; she married author Narendra Dev) as well as translations of Urdu poems composed by popular nineteenth-century poets like Ghalib, Aatish, and others. Mae West's dynamism and writings thus, help us read Indian cinema in a broader context. Though her life and works are unique in its own way and are not directly comparable to others, nevertheless, when we parallely read the interviews of Ruby Myers or figure out the manner in which Sita Devi (Rainey Smith) became the star of *Light of Asia* (Dir. Franz Osten, 1925), it lays bare the fact that the history of Indian cinema is yet to be thoroughly researched in terms of its many textures, and thus is waiting to be explored and thoroughly narrated.

WOMEN WRITING CINEMA

The poems of Meena Kumari (Naz), the actor and the Urdu poet, have been discussed by Tharu and Lalita.[71] While Naz was a name given to her by her husband, Kamal Amrohi, she actually rarely used it. Meena Kumari was also the popular actor of films like *Sahib Bibi Aur Ghulam* (Dir. Abrar Alvi, 1962), *Dil Ek Mandir* (Dir. C.V. Sridhar, 1963), *Phool Aur Pathar* (Dir. O.P. Ralhan, 1966), *Mere Apne* (Dir. Gulzar, 1971), and so on. The daughter of a Parsi theatre actor and a dancer, Mahjabeen Bano, known as the actor Meena Kumari, started her career at an early age and was married to the writer-director Kamal Amrohi, who had directed *Mahal* (1949) and written classic films like *Mughal-e-Azam* (Dir. K. Asif, 1960). After they were married they produced *Daera* (1953), supposedly based on their own impossible relationship laced with an intense longing, and later planned the film *Pakeezah* (1972). The film, however, took sixteen years to make, affected intermittently by their personal losses, divorce, as well as Meena Kumari's suffering which included her terminal illness (cirrhosis). While studies on star and popular cultures have read the ways in which the star persona leaks into and surfaces in the body of the text, the other concern of such theorizations has been to examine the manner in which the star body becomes a crucial aspect of the films.[72] This appears like a significant point of departure, as I argue that Meena Kumari's writings become the narrative drive of a film like *Pakeezah* as well as *Sahib Bibi Aur Ghulam*, and her bearing is woven into such cinematic texts. The excessive elements of a melodramatic setting, the use of lights, compositions, shot taking as well as characterization, rhetorical dialogues, performances, and the iconic face of the star draws heavily from Meena Kumari's life and the entire ethos of her poetry.

This section hopes to initiate a comparative and speculative study in its attempt to locate Meena Kumari in the larger oeuvre of popular Urdu poetry, by probing into the styles of iconic authors, the popular acceptance of particular motifs and ways in which she deployed them. For instance, while Meena Kumari's star persona fitted well into Amrohi's imagination—as projected in *Mahal* and *Mughal-e-Azam*—when they were separated in 1960 and were eventually divorced in 1964,[73] 'Naz' wrote the following:

Talak to de rahe ho
Nazare kahar ke saath.
Jawani bhi mere lauta do
Mehar ke saath.

(You give me divorce with rage in your eyes/
Return my youth along with my bridal-price.)

Indeed, these lines seem to resonate the remarkable lyrics written by Gulzar for his film *Ijaazat* (1987).[74] Therefore, it may be fruitful to compare Meena Kumari's works with other writers, and wonder why her works were published posthumously by Gulzar as *Tanhaa Chaand,* and was almost untraceable until recently.[75] Tharu and Lalita write,

> Though Meena Kumari did not have a formal education, she loved literature, and when she had time, read widely in poetry, taking careful notes in her diary. People are often surprised to discover that this distinguished actress and singer was also a poet who wrote under the pen name Naz.[76]

Meena Kumari's poems have startling imagery and sensitivity that repeatedly highlight her personal pain and yearning as well as the larger social conditions within which women perform (as depicted in a film like *Pakeezah*). Certain motifs like journey, or metaphors like 'light' and 'moon' or 'cage' and 'room', in addition, are repeatedly deployed from a perspective that completely subverts masculine subject positions, within which a popular section of Urdu *shaeri* operated.[77] For instance, Amir Khusro's famous lines on ethereal love (*'chap tilak sab chin'*/you take away the signs of piety), seem to come back with a difference—and from a woman's standpoint—as she writes:

> *Agaz to hota hai anjam nahin hota*
> *jab meri kahani main woh naam nahin hota.*

> There is a beginning but no end,
> when his name is absent from my story.

Though such expressions are not directly comparable, specific elements and the mood, particularly the idea of the self as an incomplete being, which is withering in love, return with an altered subject position. Ghalib's poems are also an interesting reference point.[78] He had written:

> *Ta phir na interzar mein neend aaye umr bhar,*
> *Aane ka wada kar gaye, aaye to khwab mein.*

O for the curse
Of sleepless nights,
Which I shall bear
Forever through life,
For she [had] promised to come
In one of my dreams.

This too may be juxtaposed with Meena Kumari's transcripts, though this does not mean that Ghalib's popular writings constitute the entire realm of Urdu poetry. Nevertheless, it is important to perceive ways in which specific imageries like *shamma-parwana, musafir-deewana,* and so on, circulated within popular imagination through mainstream Hindi films. Certainly, Meena Kumari's poems echo similar concerns, albeit from the point of view of a woman, who is pining through the night. In the ghazals (released posthumously through her album, 'I write, I recite', music by Khayyaam, HMV), she harps in her melancholic voice:

Puchhte ho to suno kaise basar hoti hai.
Raat khairaat ki sadqe ki sahar hoti hai.
Saans bharne ko to jeena nahin kahate yaa rab
Dil hi dukhata hai na ab aasteen tar hoti hai.
Jaise jaagi hui aankhon mein chubhen kaanch ke khwaab,
Raat is tarah diwanon ki basar hoti hai.
Gam hi dushman hai mera gam hi ko dil dhundhata hai
Ek lamhe ki judaai bhi agar hoti hai.

You ask me, how I live.
My nights pass in begging, and prayers fill in my mornings.
My God! To breathe is not to live,
My heart feels no pain, my eyes hold no tears,
As though dreams made of glass pierce my sleepless eyes,
The nights of an infatuated person is lived in these ways.
Sorrow is my enemy, and yet I look for sorrow
Even if we are separated for a moment.

In addition, in a peculiar manner, in an interview to *Filmfare* (1969) Meena Kumari had expressed similar views

The two phases and faces of Meena Kumari in Pakeezah

and said: 'I feel as if I am suspended in a vacuum, a dark void in which my whole being is so cold and desensitized that when thoughts and feelings come to me, they seem to come to someone else, and I watch the inner world of that other person as though I stand at a distance....'[79] Saheb Jaan the protagonist in *Pakeezah* experiences the same kind of dilemma of multiple selves. This courtesan and the illegitimate child of Nawab Shahbuddin, meets a stranger while travelling by a train. The unknown traveller enamoured by her beautiful (red) feet, leaves a note stating, 'your feet are beautiful do not put them on the ground'. For a courtesan, these lines—'do not put your feet on the ground'—produce its own significances. The enigmatic train traveller haunts her every night. Eventually lovelorn Saheb Jaan meets her friend Dibban, and tells her about her own tormenting love for this mysterious man, whose writing becomes the index of his presence. Meena Kumari's writings (particularly *Tanhaa Chaand*) seem to inform Saheb Jaan's utterances in such moments of despair. For instance, she had written, 'The moon is lonely, so is the sky/The heart travels the world alone/Hope is lost, and the stars are hidden/And, the stream trembles here alone'.[80] In *Pakeezah*, Saheb Jaan says,

> Since a couple of days I get this feeling that I am changing,
> As though I am embarking on an unknown journey.
> And, I am going somewhere by leaving back everything.

Saheb Jaan is slipping away from me,
And, I am being distanced from Saheb Jaan.

Furthermore, the relationship between her ideas, the film text and directorial explorations may have been reciprocal. As pointed out by Gulzar during personal conversations (in June 2013), one needs to consider the fact that Kamal Amrohi, the fabulous writer-director, momentously influenced both his as well as her writings. In this connection, I retain the distinction between Meena Kumari the writer and Meena Kumari the actor, and try to locate her writings in the larger poetic tradition. In addition, a film that was made for more than sixteen years and was released after the death of both the main actor and the cinematographer (Joseph Wirscing) seemingly has the entire history of its making written on its surface. On one hand, *Pakeezah* highlights a particular kind of poetic imageries which were lost by 1972,[81] on the other it has Meena Kumari's personal life and works inscribed on to its textual terrain, thereby producing a series of rich cross-references. For instance, Meena Kumari's devastated face and her demeanour—in the sections of the film, which was shot few months before her death or the scenes towards the end—bear the narratives of her own life, as well as the chronicles of young actors who joined the industry during that period, and whose efforts are situated on the thin margin between recognition and obscurity. For instance, in the scene after she has declared her love for the anonymous man, she is taken away in a boat by her wealthy client (Nawab). The Nawab, suggests that she appears somewhat lost to him, and tries to evoke the memory of an old poem, *'Chalte, chalte...'* The crucial extra-diegetic element in this context is that the song and the dance (*'Chalte, chalte'*) was shot in the earlier phase of the shooting, while this section, where Saheb Jaan narrates the poem, was evidently shot after Meena Kumari and Amrohi had reconciled and agreed to complete the film years later. This account of separation appears to be written into the narrative of the film as well on Meena Kumari's ravaged face, as Saheb Jaan, says, 'I remember', and hums the lines, 'While travelling I happened to meet someone en-route...'[82]

Intriguingly, the *kotha* (salon) set of the film, which is an open space, draws heavily from Mughal miniature paintings, as little doll-like dancers placed on top/background, reiterate Saheb Jaan's poses as she performs along with the song, *'Inhi logo ne...'* ('These are the people'). The dichotomies of the home and bazaar, private and public domains, personal and political realms are problematized, as the outside is seen from inner spaces, while the interiors, as it were, had no shutters and no hidden corners. The bazaar like the inner (yet open) domain becomes a site where the concerns of the *tawaif* (courtesan) are enunciated. Within this trope, while the film begins with Nargis (Saheb Jaan's mother) escaping marriage, in order to save her lover's reputation, towards the end, Saheb Jaan (renamed Pakeezah) too suffers a comparable situation and runs away from the marriage scene in her attempt to protect the status of Salim (the man of her imaginings). Afterwards, on returning to the desolate kotha, a visibly distraught Saheb Jaan says:

> 'I am a dead body ...
> and this bazaar is a graveyard ...
> These mansions are our tombs ...
> [and] and our coffins are left open ...
> I am a restless dead body, who is lured by life repeatedly.
> ... .'

However, Amrohi's plotting may be further problematized as one examines the dense *mise-en-scene*, where every space is loaded with connotations. Thus, the complication of the film begins in a graveyard (this is also the place where Saheb Jaan is born); moreover, we observe Nargis—also played by Meena Kumari—writing her thoughts in this location. Effectively, on-screen we see Meena Kumari's (hand) writing and her anguish.

Issues of respectability and legitimacy, as well as the function of tawaif as the writer are also underscored towards the end of the film, when Saheb Jaan is invited to dance at Salim's engagement. She sings mournfully by questioning God, and dances frantically on broken glass. Her blood, splattered on her family courtyard, not only highlights her yearning for the lover, it effectually brings up the subject of her parenthood and that she indeed was born out of love and 'noble' blood. Eventually, Salim's engagement is terminated; and, the film ends in the kotha, where Salim arrives along with the dead body of his uncle/Saheb Jaan's father, Shahbuddin (in a coffin), to take away the bride (Saheb Jaan) from the bazaar-kotha, which was also her home. Despite this happy ending of sorts, the last shot of the film, and the image of a lonesome young girl (comparable to the kite used in the film) looking out into nothingness complicates the overall plotting by demonstrating the point that the issue is not resolved as yet.

This figure, appropriately reminds one of Ratan Bai whose anecdote is lost and thus been erased from mainstream histories of Indian cinema. Personal stories of performers joining the film industry from disparate fields including the theatrical stage, gramophone industries and the kothas accentuate the rich accounts of performance cultures and its connections with cinema. The inter-textuality, moreover, both in the realm of visual arts as well as within the ambit of literature, makes the film a thick terrain of cross-references, where Meena Kumari's persona and poems seem to thicken the multi-layered text. Indeed, *Pakeezah* narrates a weightier history of cinema, which is deeply connected to the lives of performing artists, different modes of performances, various forms of utterances and gender politics. For instance, about the *Choti Bahu* (played by Meena Kumari) of *Sahib Bibi Aur Ghulam,* Arun Khopar writes,

Who or what Chhoti Bahu?
    She is proud and falls at her husband's feet. She is chaste and becomes her husband's prostitute. With no help but

liquor at the end she is pure as driven snow.... Voluptuous, marble-skinned, ebony-haired, dressed in gold and silver, she has unfathomable eyes, and a voice that arouses every pore in the skin. ...She is the life force irresistibly drawn to its own death.[83]

Though Khopar talks about the 'voluptuousness', 'the ebony hair' and particularly the grain of the voice of the character Choti Bahu, in reality, these are Meena Kumari's own. This is especially audible as one hears Meena Kumari's lament-like rendition of her own poems in the album *I write, I recite*. By the time *Sahib Bibi Aur Ghulam* was made Meena Kumari was suffering heavily from a 'drinking' condition, and the scene in which she forces Bhootnath to get her drinks reverberates with Meena Kumari's own despair. Nevertheless, my interest is not in the events in Meena Kumari's life, but in her 'star persona', which is deeply associated with her writings, longings, as well as the 'affect' her image produces via major cinematic texts. Such close reading of the poems and the film texts highlights the ways in which gender studies becomes a powerful device to revisit film history and its connections with wider political–cultural history. It underlines further the value of popular material and the processes through which it may open up new paradoxes.

WOMEN CONCEIVING CINEMA

This volume interrogates the Indian Cinematograph Committee Report (ICCR, 1927–28), where the very notion of cinema is under the shadow of doubt (see Chapter 4). In fact, the first attempts to debate on cinema emerged through the ICCR commissioned by the empire. The Committee was designed to probe into the film market vis-à-vis the inroads of American films in the Indian market. The interim period between the two world wars was essentially marked with an extraordinary conflict over colonies in pursuit of economic and political control. In this context, the rapidly changing technology driven art form—cinema—with an inadequately assessed market potential, created apprehensions among film entrepreneurs. The anxieties, in fact, were at its peak during the Second World War, with a number of British and American journals publishing reports on the production–distribution–exhibition conditions of the Indian film industry (as well as other colonies).[84]

In principle, the ICCR was devised to produce a sanction to control the production and exhibition of films made by Indians, just as it hoped to encourage the growth of British films. The Committee (comprising three Indians and three Englishmen) examined the effectiveness of the industry, while the questions addressed to respectable subjects of the country hovered around moral issues and an undefined logic of quality. Members of the legislative committee, police officers, judges, professors, political leaders, actors, producers, filmmakers and others were interviewed.[85] For instance, The Indian Cinematograph Committee Questionnaire included the following questions:

5. Are Indian-produced films, depicting Indian life, readily available to exhibitors? If so,
   (a) are they of good quality?
   (b) are they popular?
   (c) is it ordinarily less or more profitable to show an Indian than a Western film? Can you cite any examples of successful Indian films?
6. (a) Do you think that films of Indian life, topical Indian news and scenes (with Indian actors) depicting stories from the national literature history and mythology, would be more popular with Indian audiences than the prevalent Western films?
   (b) Of such films what kind would appeal most strongly
       (1) to the educated classes,

| Introducing Voices and Verses

(2) to the illiterate population?... [the extracts from the ICCR documents are represented as they appear in the original]

More importantly, Part II dealing with 'Social Aspects and Control' comprised the following queries:

24. (a) Do you consider that any class of films exhibited in this country has a demoralising or otherwise injurious effect upon the public?
    (b) Is there a general circulation of immoral or criminally suggestive films?
    (c) In your opinion what class of film is harmful? To whom is it harmful? In what way is it harmful?
    (d) Consider specifically whether censorship is adequate in the cases of
        (1) 'Sex' films
        (2) 'Crime' films.
    (e) Do you consider there has been any increase of crime in your Province due to the Cinema?
    (f) Support your statements wherever possible by instances within your personal knowledge.
25. Do you consider that the differences in social customs and outlook between the West and the East necessitate special consideration in the censorship of films in this country? [as appears in the original]

While one of the key concerns of the Committee was to strengthen the censorship policies, the series of questions pitched at the interviewees also included the following:

33. Would a strict censorship –
    (a) interfere unreasonably with the recreations of the people?
    (b) involve a falling off in the attendance at Cinemas?
    (c) unduly interfere with the freedom required for the artistic and inspirational development?

34. (a) Do you advocate the replacement of the present Provincial Boards of Censors by a single Central Board?
    (1) If so why?
    (2) Would this cause any inconvenience to the Trade?
    (3) How would such a Central Board be constituted?
    (4) Where should it be situated?
    (b) Or, would you advocate a Central Board in addition to the Provincial Boards?
    (c) If you advocate a Central Board working either alone or with the Provincial Boards, how would you regulate the relationship between the various Boards and the Central and the Local Governments?
    (d) How would such a Board or Boards be financed?

35. (a) Is the present constitution of the Provincial Boards (of which at least half the Members must, under the law, be non-officials) satisfactory?
    (b) Would you prefer a whole-time experienced well-paid officer as Censor at each centre, to be assisted by an Advisory Board of non-officials?

36. (a) Do you think that the present system (prevailing at Bombay and Calcutta) under which films are ordinarily examined by inspectors subordinate to the Board is satisfactory? Are such inspectors sufficiently well qualified for the work? What sort of qualifications are essential?
    (b) Or do you think that all films should be examined by Members of the Board? If so do you consider that gentlemen of suitable standing will be available who would be prepared to devote sufficient time to the examination of films for a reasonable remuneration? [as appears in the original]

While such pointed queries demonstrate the overall concerns of the British government, however, contrary to the expectations of the government, which was to offer preferential treatment to British films, the Committee instead demanded a programme to support Indian producers. It recommended that Indian producers should be able to take loans from public funds (though the English committee members disapproved of this) and exhibition conditions should improve. It also suggested that a new department should set up with functions ranging from training to technical maintenance, to organizing competitions for productions and screenplay. Moreover, as far as issues of 'good' cinema were concerned, Western films were accepted, while censorship was encouraged. The Report also suggested that cinema should be used as means of mass education. More significantly, besides what the Report declared, what becomes apparent through an analysis of the interviews was an intention to connect the technology of cinema with larger debates on Indian modernity, and examine the possibilities of cinema becoming the bearer of Indian modernity. Cinema was described as an art as well as a thriving industry that supported hundreds of technicians and workers. Barring a few critics, cinema was largely recognized as a positive and valuable agency, which could possibly realize the nation-building project.[86] It is in this context that I examine the remarkable interviews of Ruby Myers, Patience Cooper, Sita Devi and others.

Ruby Myers née Sulochana was one of the biggest stars of the silent era. Apparently, she was the highest paid actor of the period, and her salary was higher than the Governor of Bombay's. She was associated with Kohinoor and Imperial Film Co., and was popularly known as both the Queen of Romance and Jungle Queen. Often she was teamed with the popular male actor of the period, D. Billimoria. In the film *Wild Cat of Bombay* (1927), she played eight different roles (which included both male and female masquerades). Kaushik Bhaumik writes:

Sulochana was thus pushing the envelope of the cosmopolitanism espoused by the industry that had begun with her career with Kohinoor. Her films tended to project an overall atmosphere of glamour and an aura of the fashionable, both of which conveyed a sense of the daring and of the experimental. Dress and on-screen lifestyle fed off each other to underscore the persona of a modern working woman fully in charge of her life and at ease in the public sphere and this could be as attractive for men as it was for women.[87]

Curiously, in the interview cited in this volume, Ruby Myers claims that she worked in the 'telephone office' before she joined the industry. Thus, her films like *Telephone-ni Taruni* (1926) and so on seem to be drawn from her own professional background and vice versa. While her peak ended with the advent of the talkies, she continued to be associated with films, initially performed in the remakes of her own films, and later played character roles in *Anarkali* (Dir. Nandalal Jaswantlal, 1953), *Haqeeqat* (Dir. Chetan Anand, 1973), *Julie* (Dir. Sethumadhavan, 1975), and so on. In the interview with the ICC discussed here, Ruby Myers responded accordingly to the following question:

Chairman: And what do you think should be done to make it [film-acting] more attractive?

A: Well, I think if we were financed properly, if there were some technical improvements and if there were some way of getting fairly good stories—if we could get stories like Tagore's and some others, which I know would appeal to the educated classes—our stories at present are very poor. We want better stories either taken from the ancient books or good modern authors.

Q. You want more literary effort in that direction?

A. Yes. And, of course, the studios are quite good in the present conditions. That is, things being what they are, they are quite good.

Q. Although you would like to have them improved, you would not insist on it at the present stage? What I want to know really is whether for the educated classes and also for girls of good family the conditions in the studios are sufficiently attractive. ...

A. Well, what I see of them they are very respectable company. They behave very well and they work very well.

Q. Although they may have come from the lower class?

A. I don't think they have come from a very low class. Most of them are very very good company.[88]

While Ruby Myers goes on to talk about the production conditions, salary of the stars, (the poor) technology deployed to make films, and so on, it is also engaging to consider that she considers Tagore (who apparently belonged to Bengal and the bhadralok domain) as a valuable source for film texts. Similarly, Patience Cooper was associated with Madan Theatres during the silent era. She acted in films like *Nala Damayanti* (1922), while her last film *Kapalkundala*, ran to packed houses during the same time.[89] Therefore, while concluding, I wish to underline some of the paradoxes of history and refer back to the point where Charu in the exposition of Ray's adaptation of Tagore, takes out the book *Kapalkundala*. Curiously, when Sir Haroon Jaffer from ICC enquired, 'You mix with Indian ladies also in this cinema company?' Cooper replied the following:

A. We do work with them.

Q. How do you find them, are they of respectable family?

A. Away from the studio, I don't know them at all.

Q. You don't know their private life?

A. No.

Q. But when you meet them you think they come from respectable families.

A. Yes, they seem all right; they seem quite nice.

Q. I want to know about the respectability of their family. They behave all right in the studio?

A. They behave all right.

Mr. Neogy [of ICC]: Do you know Bengali?

A. No.

Q. When you have to interpret certain sentiments for the film you have to depend upon the directions given by the director?

A. Yes, he explains everything in English.

Q. You don't find it at all inconvenient to interpret those things?

A. No.[90]

Intriguingly, if both Ray and Chatterjee were evoking Bankim Chandra (as well as Tagore) to examine the bhadralok predicaments, a close reading of these oral evidences illustrate the complexities of the public sphere, which is copious with cultural cross-references and is not restricted to one tendency. Issues of cinema, gender, work, class, communities, language, sexuality and everyday practices combined to produce the rich texture of political-cultural differences of the period. While Madan Theatres were criticized for infusing a 'Parsi taste' and 'cheap thrills' into Bengali culture and sophistication, somewhat ironically it was the Eurasian actors like Cooper and others, who were actually playing out bhadralok dilemmas in the public domain. It was only later, in the 1930s that the bhadromahila (like Promila Devi and Sadhana Bose) began to appear on screen, and often performed as well as choreographed dances in oriental tales like *Alibaba* (Dir. Modhu Bose, 1937).[91] Certainly, during this time, 'women' were in a decisive way conceiving cinema, and not merely commenting on them. In fact, they were producing a cinematic sensibility that would remain influential for years to come. To use Kanan Devi's words: 'The unhappy times that we had to go through in the early days of the Bengali cinema have not been entirely wasted. We could remain a witness to such successful changes in our own lifetime.'[92]

It is crucial to examine the function of women and their knotty gendered positions when they became part of a larger patriarchal structure like the Censor Board and framed regulations for cinema as well as for film posters. It may thus be suggested that such 'Voices' become powerful evidences of a larger and a long-drawn struggle of several female actors (or workers) who hoped to survive and create ruptures within the broader political–cultural paradigm. Furthermore, the disparate forms of writings and utterances (interviews, letters, as well as articles, biographies, screenplays and poems), written over a period of fifty years in different languages, lay bare extremely varied modes of expressions in terms of their choice of caustic words and sharp wit, or emotional excesses and flowery remarks. By and large, women authors (writing about cinema and/or writing films), however, use a self-reflexive tone; therefore, in their attempt to talk about their own lives and work, they mostly comment on very complicated social issues. Eventually, Kanan Devi, Ratan Bai and others' accounts in reality tell us more than we acknowledge about New Theatres, just as Ruby Myers, Patience Cooper and Sita Devi's testimonies throw light on the functioning of the film industry during the twenties and the thirties. Likewise, Mrs. Ansell's educational film on poultry farming shows us a different trajectory of Indian cinema. It is only in the recent past that with the opening up of the colonial film archive that a range of documentaries and documentations of the colonial period have come within our purview.[93] Such films demonstrate the influences of British documentaries, as well as the connections between reform issues and realism as a form, that would become perceptible between the forties and the sixties. Mrs. Ansell's role, thus, becomes momentous from this perspective. Indeed, such interpretations compel us to *revisit* the 'history' of Indian cinemas, which is yet to thoroughly historicize its own industrial past.

NOTES

1   Also see Satyajit Ray's *Speaking of Films* (New Delhi: Penguin India, 2005) translated from *Bishaye Chalachitra* (1976), on the issues of adaptation, borrowing and transformation in the context of *Charulata*.

2   See my article on gender and work in 'Notes on the City and Goddesses: Indrani, Nita, Arati', in *Proceedings of the Seminar on Post-Independence Bengali Cinema* (Kolkata: Gurudas College, December 2007): 39–51.

3   This scene literarily shows Amal storming into her life. Her lazy afternoon is disturbed as the April storms suddenly break in, blowing off the saris and perturbing the caged bird. At this point, Amal enters with an umbrella in his hand and shouts, 'Have you read *Anandamath* [by Bankim Chandra Chattopadhyay]?', which appears like a foretelling of a rather complicated chronicle.

4   It is interesting to revisit the seminal nineteenth-century essay by Bankim Chandra. '*Prachina ebang Navina*', initially published in *Bangadarshan*, which brings up the question of how the ordinary woman like 'Pachi, Rami, Madhi' after being educated in English, were getting disconnected from their own cultural roots and becoming lazy, uncaring, self-indulgent, disrespectful and even transgressing 'their limits'. '*Navina* is like a *babu*...,' wrote Bankim Chandra. Not that he was totally against women's liberation (he reminds us of the role of women in the French Revolution in this article; moreover, the female characters of his novels were very powerful indeed), however, he particularly questions the issue of 'English education'. Nevertheless, what is truly remarkable about this debate, are the three rejoinders published in *Bangadarshan* (supposedly written by Bankim Chandra himself, under different pen names), and the language of these letters are laced with sarcasm, wit and panache. While, Chandikasundari Devi, criticizes the babu referring to them as the worshippers of the bottle and not the idol, Lakshmani Devi, writes in a sarcastic tone that 'we accept we have many vices—firstly we are women, then Bengali, then of lower caste and from

far off places—surely we will have vices...', and Rasamayi Devi following the same line, asks the author to switch roles with a woman. Overall, each letter criticizes the 'anonymous' author and connects ideas of gender, class, caste and reform movements in multiple ways. While Partha Chatterjee (*The Nation and Its Fragments: Colonial and Postcolonial Histories*, New Delhi: Oxford University Press, 1994) gives us his pathbreaking analysis of these issues, Ray as a matter of fact, problematizes the role of navina-prachina as well as that of the bhadralok through his film as early as 1964.

5   See Moinak Biswas (ed.), *Apu and After, Re-visiting Ray's Cinema* (Calcutta: Seagull Books, 2006).

6   'I shall explain politics to you,' he had said earlier.

7   See Moinak Biswas 'Bengali Film Debates: The Literary Liaison Revisited', *Journal of the Moving Image* 1 (1999): 1–13.

8   Soumitra Chattopadhyay in his interviews has repeatedly suggested that his handwriting was transformed permanently after Ray inspired him to practise calligraphy to acquire the stylized handwriting of Amal.

9   It is important to note how Ray introduces contemptuous responses of the prachina or Mandar, which includes her conspicuous gaze, as she scornfully observes and smiles while Charu and Amal debate in the garden. Moreover, in the sequence where Bhupati celebrates the victory of the Liberals (in England), his friends show him Charu's writing. A baffled Bhupati negotiates a situation like this with some difficulty. In fact, this sequence brings up the tensions between ghar and bahir, and the ways in which women's writings were received in the bhadralok public sphere.

10 The idea of word play is common in Ray, as seen in films like *Aranyer Din Ratri* (1970).

11 Note, in the first sequence Charu picks up a copy of *Kapalkundala*. *Kapalkundala* (1866) is a tragic love story between the innocent and unnurtured Kapalkundala and Nabakumar, whose love is destroyed after their marriage. Also see n89.

Bishabriksha (1873) was the first novel of Chattopadhyay to appear in a serialized form in *Bangadarshan*. It is an intense story of love and longing, with multiple sub-plots. At the centre of the plot is Kunda, the widow, whose beauty destroys her lover(s).

12 While Amal apparently ignores her passionate expression, she continues, '*Aar Bouthan? Bouthan, baaje? Bisree? Behaya?*' (Meaning, 'And, me? Am I bad, unpleasant, and brazen?'); 'Bouthan' refers to sister-in-law.

13 Cited from *The Partha Chatterjee Omnibus: Nationalist Thought and the Colonial World, The Nation and Its Fragments, A Possible India* (New Delhi: Oxford University Press, 2002).

14 An obvious reference to Tagore's *Ghare Baire* (1916), which was adapted by Ray in 1984.

15 Chatterjee, *The Nation and Its Fragments*:120.

16 While Sumit Sarkar in 'The Women's Question in Nineteenth-Century Bengal', and *Recasting Women: Essays in Indian Colonial History* (New Delhi: Kali for Women, 1989) present a different inquisition, a more recent book by Sarmistha Dutta Gupta, titled *Identities and Histories, Women's Writing and Politics in Bengal* (Kolkata: Stree, 2010) brings up startling new material that may challenge Chatterjee's theorization. Further, in the chapter on melodrama and Debaki Bose, in my Ph.D. dissertation, 'The New Theatres Ltd.: "The Cathedral of Culture" and the House of the Popular', I show how the new woman as described by Chatterjee as, 'quite the reverse of the "common" woman, who was coarse, vulgar, loud, quarrelsome, devoid of superior moral sense, sexually promiscuous, subjected to brutal physical oppression by males...', may be contested. Also see Kumkum Sangari's *Politics of the Possible: Essays on Gender, History, Narrative, Colonial English* (Delhi: Tulika, 1999).

17 Chatterjee, *The Nation and Its Fragments*:128. This question of bhadromahila is also addressed in P. C. Barua's *Adhikar* (1938), which is plotted around the rich–poor, respectability–illegitimacy, bhadromahila–common woman dichotomy. Radha, the illegitimate and poor half-sister of Indira (Jamuna Barua), eventually reclaims her social rights as well as Indira's love (Nikhilesh). In a particular sequence, when Radha questions Indira, her value system (*bhadrata*) and asks, 'That he [Nikhilesh] never loves you, or hugs you or kisses...don't you want all that?' Surely, for the bhadromahila this appears very vulgar, while for Radha, 'desire is central to her existence'. Indira thus, replies, 'her position doesn't allow her to cry' (or express).

18 'The Women and the Nation', in Chatterjee, *The Nation and Its Fragments*: 139.

19 Ibid.

20 Susie Tharu and K. Lalita (eds.), *Women Writing in India, 600 B.C. to the Present*, 2 vols. (New Delhi: Oxford University Press, 1992).

21 Ibid.: 34. The second volume features poetry, fiction, drama and autobiography by 73 writers born after 1905. These works bring into the scope of literary discussion a new range of women's experiences and their responses to society, politics, desire, marriage, procreation, aging and death.

22 Tharu and Lalita (eds.), *Women Writing in India*.

23 Christine Gledhill, *Gender Meets Genre in Postwar Cinemas* (Baltimore: University of Illinois Press, 2012): 278.

24 See Samita Sen, 'Wives, Widows and Prostitutes', in *Women and Labour in Late Colonial India: The Bengal Jute Industry* (Cambridge University Press, 1999).

25 See Rosie Thomas, 'Not Quite (Pearl) White: Fearless Nadia, Queen of Stunts', R. Kaur and A. J. Sinha (eds.), *Bollyworld: Popular Indian Cinema through a Transnational Lens* (New Delhi: SAGE, 2005); and Neepa Majumdar's more recent work, *Wanted Cultured Ladies Only!, Female Stardom and Cinema in India, 1930s–1950s* (New Delhi: Oxford University Press, 2010).

26 See Ann Kaplan (ed.), *Film and Feminism* (Oxford: Oxford University Press, 2000); Molly Haskell, *From Reverence to Rape: The Treatment of Women in the Movies* (Chicago: The University of Chicago Press, 1987), Mary Ann Doane, *Femmes Fatales: Feminism, Film Theory, Psychoanalysis* (New York: Routledge, 1991). Jennifer M. Bean and Diane Negra (eds.), *Feminist Reader in Early Cinema* (Durham: Duke University Press, 2002); Judith Butler, *Bodies That Matter: On the Discursive Limits of 'Sex'* (New York/London: Routledge, 1993); Laura Mulvey, 'Visual Pleasure and Narrative Cinema', in *Screen* 16 (3), 1975: 6–18; Jackie Stacey, *Star Gazing: Hollywood Cinema and Female Spectatorship* (London: Routledge, 1993); Antonia Lant et al. (eds.), *Red Velvet Seat: Women's Writings on the First Fifty Years of Cinema* (London: Verso, 2006).

27 See Vicki Callahan, *Reclaiming the Archive: Feminism and Film History* (Michigan: Wayne State University, 2010).

28 See *Musings*, translated from Telegu, *Nalo Nenu* in 1993 (Chennai: P.B.R. Publications, 2000).

29 See http://www.thehindu.com/mp/2005/12/27/stories/ 2005122700900400.htm; last accessed on 25 July 2014.

30 See *I, Durga Khote* (translated from Marathi, *Mee, Durga Khote* by Shanta Gokhale) (New Delhi: Oxford University Press, 1976); republished in 2007: xxiv.

31 *I, Durga Khote.* 69.

32 In my book *New Theatres Ltd., the Emblem of Art, the Picture of Success* (Pune: NFAI, 2009), I have written about the decline of the studios during the period 1942–47, which were deeply connected to the Partition and the communal riots that preceded the event. While films continued to be made, the rationing of the raw stock and black marketing made it almost impossible for the big studios to sustain their productions. The disintegration of the feudalistic studio system, the advent of Nehruvian modernity and 'new' Bombay cinemas with rising 'auteurs' like Raj Kapoor and Mehboob Khan eventually became the key problems for deliberations.

33 See *I, Durga Khote.*

34 Amiya Bagchi, in *Private Investment in India, 1900–1939* (Cambridge: Cambridge University Press, 1972), while discussing the major industries in India like cotton, jute, cement, sugar, paper, iron, steel, and so on, does not bring up the question of cinema (clearly because of its dubious status, unevenness, lack of records and constant flow of black money, and so on) though journals of the film industry somewhat arguably and polemically upheld it as an industry larger than the cement industry (in association with the paper industry). Moreover, in several films including *President* (Nitin Bose, 1938), problems of the industries became the key concerns.

35 *Sabare Ami Nomi* (Kolkata: M. C. Sarkar and Sons, 1973).

36 For a discussion on the films see 'Early Indian Talkies: Voice, Performance and Aura', *Journal of the Moving Image* 6 (December 2007): 39–61.

37 For instance, a poem '*Amader Troyi*'/Our Three (by Raghunath Kundu) in *Chitrapanji* (Bengali) 1938, mentions the popular female actors of the period (Jyotsna Gupta, Chhaya Devi and Kananbala).

38 Also see Soumitra Chattopadhyay's interview of Kananbala in '*Rabibaroyari*', *Ei Samaye*, 4 August 2013: 2–4.

39 In *Chitrapanji* 4(6), 1934: 266–68.

40 Ibid.

41 See my Ph.D. thesis, 'The Emblem of Art', in *New Theatres Ltd*.

42 In May 1939, K.A. Abbas wrote an article titled 'These Three! Prabhat–New Theatres–Bombay Talkies' in *Film India*, presenting a comparative history of these three studios, located in different regions of India. Abbas begins the article with quotes from imagined viewers who describe Prabhat Film Co'.s films as 'grand', but for 'Maharashtrians only', the New Theatres' films as 'beautiful', but only for intellectuals, and Bombay Talkies as 'good' or as 'bad' as Hollywood. Abbas further elaborates on the 'Prabhat touch' and issues of progressive ideals and reform as well as realism existing even in the mythological productions of the period.

43 Madan Theatres Ltd. built Calcutta's first theatre in India and dominated the scene for about thirty years. Around 1925 and 1926 all Bengali films were Madans' productions. By 1927, Madans' distribution chain controlled half of India's theatre halls. They owned about 172 theatre halls and picked up half of the national profits. Their exhibition chain extended to Burma and Ceylon (Sri Lanka) and they were the primary company to import films from Hollywood. By the thirties, however, this mammoth production–distribution–exhibition house was already losing much of its ground.

Ahindra Chowdhury wrote in Gouranga Prasad Ghosh, *Sonar Daag* (Calcutta: Yogamaya Prakashani, 1982: 119), 'in 1929, I was forced to quit the Madans.... The Madan Co. was no longer the same. They were indebted to many....' Similarly, Madhu Bose wrote (*Sonar Daag*:130), 'I was shocked, as I entered Madans' office that day. Rustomji was excited and was shouting...how one can save Madans from this disaster....'

Around 1930, the Madans hastily tried to reorganize themselves. Earlier in the late 1920s, J. J. Madan, son of J. F. Madan, had visited New York, and as he saw *Jazz Singer* (1927) and witnessed the frenzy around the singing stars, he got an immediate indication of changing production relations. 'J. Madan caught the fever' (Eric Barnouw and S. Krishnaswamy, *Indian Film*, second edition, New Delhi: Oxford University Press, 1980: 65) and Madans imported R.C.A. sound machines, constructed sound compatible studios and recorded scenes from popular theatres like *Alamgir, Shajahan, Iraner Rani, Mrinalini*. They promptly conducted voice tests in their endeavour to re-launch themselves in the sound era. Eminent theatre personalities like Ahindra Chowdhury, Durgadas Bandyopadhyay, singer K.C. Dey, actresses like Patience Cooper, Violet Cooper, Sita Devi stood before the microphone to pass the test of times. On 13 March 1931, Madans screened about 30 short films in Crown Theatre, Calcutta. The Imperial Movietone, Bombay, however, finally made it to the history books, as it released *Alam Ara*, the first full-length feature film on 14 August 1931. In 1932, Madans did fairly good business, yet in 1933 they produced only two films. This volume includes interviews of Patience Cooper, as well as of Sita Devi (Rainey Smith) et al. (see Chapter 4).

44 B. Jha, *B. N. Sircar, Monograph* (Calcutta: published by NFAI, Pune, in association with Seagull Books, 1990).

45 Rani Burra, *Film India; Looking Back—1896–1960* (New Delhi: The Directorate of Film Festivals, 1981): 55.

46 On one hand, Madans were criticized for monopolistic approach in the ways in which they controlled distribution and exhibition; on the other, they were the prime players in importing cheaply made American films to the Indian market and thereby effectively producing a taste for a specific popular form.

47 Cited in B. Jha, *B. N. Sircar.* 33.

48 As a matter of fact, some books in Bengali (for example, Gouranga Prasad Ghosh, *Sonar Daag*) narrate stories of such passages through cinema and consequently imply various kinds of exploitations that the actors might have experienced.

49 Cited in *Journal of the Moving Image* 9, December 2010: 33.

50 I am particularly referring to Sharmistha Gooptu's *Bengali Cinema: An Other Nation* (New Delhi: Roli Books, 2010).

51 Such details were presented by Samik Bandyopadhyay, *Indian Cinema: Contemporary Perspectives from the Thirties* (Jamshedpur: Celluloid Chapter, 1993).

52 Cited from the article titled 'Should Respectable Ladies Join the Films' in *Filmland*, September 1931.

53 In the interviews of the actors cited (from the ICCR, 1927–28) in this volume, the problem of respectability comes up persistently. Also see Chapter 2.

54 *Chitrapanji*, 6 (9), June–July, 1937.

55 *Chitrapanji*, 5 (10), July–August, 1936. *Puja* issue/*sharadiya sankhya* (published on the occasion of Durga Puja, the most important festival celebrated by Hindu Bengalis. To mark this occasion periodicals have special publications).

56 Neepa Majumdar, *Wanted Cultured Ladies Only!, Female Stardom and Cinema in India, 1930s–1950s* (New Delhi: Oxford University Press, 2010).

57 See my anthology *Aural Films, Oral Cultures, Essays on Cinema from the Early Sound Era* (Kolkata: Jadavpur University Press, 2012).

58 One may make a similar argument with musical influences as well. See Madhuja Mukherjee, 'The Architecture of Songs and Music: Soundmarks of Bollywood, a Popular Form and Its Emergent Texts', *Screen Sound Journal* 3 (November 2012): 9–34.

59 *Chitrapanji*, September 1937.

60 *Chitrapanji*, April 1938.

61 *Chitrapanji*, May 1938.

62 *Chitrapanji*, September 1938.

63 *Chitrapanji*, March 1935.

64 The translated article appeared in Bengali in *Chitrapanji*, 4(4), 1934: 202–04. Also see Chapter 3.

65 The elaborate courtroom sequence from *I'm No Angel* (1933) has been referred in Chapter 3.

66 See http://www.brainyquote.com/quotes/authors/m/mae_west.html; last accessed on 25 July 2014.

67 See http://womenshistory.about.com/od/quotes/a/mae_west.htm; last accessed on 25 July 2014.

68 About this she said that while during the day she was with the Paramount, during the night she was with the 'fox'.

69 US: Manor Books.

70 In *I'm No Angel* she retorts, 'It's not the men in your life that count, it's the life in your men.'

71 Tharu and Lalita (eds.), *Women Writing in India*, 2.

72 See seminal works by Christine Gledhill, *Stardom: Industry of Desire* (New York: Routledge, 1991) and Richard Dyer's *Heavenly*

Bodies: Film Stars and Society (New York/London: Routledge, 2004), besides the latter's classic study *Stars* first published in 1979 (London: British Film Institute).

73 Curiously in *Mahal*, Amrohi shows how the protagonist had not seen his wife's face, instead he remembered her hands. Interestingly, Ghalib wrote, 'Her hand and arm/Be protected from harm of all evil eyes/But why should you look/At the wounds of my heart/Deep..., so deep?'

74 Gulzar wrote for *Ijaazat* (1987):
Mera kuch samaan tumhare paas pada hai/savan ke kuch bheege bheege din rakhe hain/
aur mere ik khat mein lipti raat padi hai/woh raat bhulaa do, mera woh saamaan lauta do/...
(Roughly: My things lie with you,/The wet monsoons days,/And a night wrapped in a letter,/Make me forget that night; return to me my things that lie with you...).

75 The new compilation *Meena Kumari the Poet: A Life beyond Cinema* (New Delhi: Roli Books, 2014) presents translations (by Noorul Hasan) of some of her poems and ghazals. The volume, however, presents her poetic endeavours as a disconnect from her cinematic persona. Moreover, the translation and specifically gendering of her poems like '*Pakeezah*' (p. 54) meaning the 'pure' (Pak) one as 'the virgin', appear problematic in the context of this volume.

76 Tharu and Lalita (eds.), *Women Writing in India* 2: 364.

77 The other example would be Faiz Ahmed Faiz who wrote extremely romantic yet political poems that seem to challenge the existing paradigms. For instance, Faiz writes,
Uht rahi hai kahin qurbat se/Teri saans ki aanch/
Apni khushbu mein sulagti hui/Maddham maddham.
(From somewhere very close/rises the warmth of your breath/smoldering in its own aroma)/bit by bit.

78 Ghalib also writes poems addressed to God; moreover, the gender role particularly within Sufi tradition is somewhat undefined. However, authors like Meena Kumari and Faiz complicate as well as locate such writings in the contemporary context.

79 From Tharu and Latita (eds.). *Women Writing in India* 2: 364.

80 Ghalib had written, 'This heart of mine/wayward and wild/ enemy of peace/condemning me/to endless wandering'.

81 A specific kind of lyricism is produced through the settings, diffused lights and the overall mise-en-scene.

82 A similar argument may be made about the song '*Chalo dildar chalo...*'

83 Cited from *Journal of Arts and Ideas*, January–March 1983: 62.

84 An article in *Sight and Sound* (1936, Autumn) asserted that 'British films should be distributed everywhere, ...otherwise while we are still yawning and stretching after a long, self-satisfied sleep, the market and a British Empire may be lost to America.'

85 For a discussion on ICCR and the question of class, see Manishita Dass, 'The Crowd Outside the Lettered City: Imagining the Mass Audience in 1920s India', *Cinema Journal*, Summer, 48.4, 2009. Also, Priya Jaikumar, *Cinema at the End of Empire: A Politics of Transition in Britain and India* (Durham: Duke University Press, 2006) for 'procedure and findings'.

86 Curiously Mahatma Gandhi (ICCR 4, 56) refused to sit for an interview and instead sent in a note saying:
Even if I was so minded, I should be unfit to answer your questionnaire as I have never been to a cinema. But even to an outsider, the evil that has done and is doing is patent. The good, if it has done any at all, remains to be proved.

87 'Sulochana: Clothes, Stardom and Gender in Early Indian Cinema', Rachel Moseley (ed.), *Fashioning Film Stars, Dress, Culture, Identity* (London: BFI Publishing, 2005): 88–97.

88 ICCR 5: 1–7; also see Chapter 4.

89 *Kapalkundala* is an archetypal plot that deals with images of the eternal 'feminine' (emerging out of nowhere), and the 'outside' that is transported on to familial spaces, even as it includes travels and narratives of Islamic conquests, Hindu revivalism and so on. In short, it represents the fears and aspirations of the period. It became a prototype of Bengali nationalism, and has been adapted several times, including versions made in 1952 and in 1981.

90 ICCR 2: 894–97.

91 Undoubtedly, with *Alibaba* Bengali cinema had its first large-scale spectacle with horses, huge sets, massive orchestration (by T. Fritzpolo) and elaborate dance sequences (choreographed by Sadhana Bose). Commenting on the decadence of the nawabi

system, one of the most memorable sequences in the film is the one in which Marjina seduces the very elderly cobbler, Baba Mustafa. Indeed, Baba Mustafa's excitement (and the famous lines 'Aha, what are you doing, Bibi Saheb?') juxtaposed with Marjina's stylized gestures in the manner in which she lies on his bed, make this scene one of the most iconic one within Indian cinema. Clearly (bhadromahila) Sadhana Bose's performance in the film is a curious critique of the bhadralok predicaments. The stylized acting, choreographed dances, tableau sequences and comic interjections by Abdullah (played by Modhu Bose) produce value-loaded moments for Indian cinema. Especially significant is the last sequence of the film, which deploys ambient sound (first of its kind which creates the sense of humming by the bandits hiding inside the barrels) and the manner in which it uses engaging inter-cuts between dancers performing before the bandits and Marjina executing a mass killing (in order to rescue her master). The climax of the film becomes forceful at the point when Marjina dashes in with an oriental headgear and performs with a knife. This sequence publicized in colour, seems to have circulated within the Bengali public spheres for decades, culminating into the (only) colour sequence of the black and white film *Marjina-Abdullah* (Dir. Dinen Gupta, 1973). There have been various adaptations of the *Alibaba* narrative in other languages as well.

92 *Sabare Ami Nomi*, 57.
93 Someswar Bhowmik writes:
The Indian Cinematography Act 1918 (Act II of 1918), which finally evolved out of the said Bill, paved the way for the omniscient system of film censorship. The exhibition of films was brought under close supervision of government officials, vested with statutory powers. Two things were made mandatory: securing a license from the local civil authorities by any prospective exhibitor; and compulsory pre-censorship of each and every film, whether produced indigenously or imported from abroad; this was done to ascertain its suitability for public exhibition.

Besides, there were provisions for administrative prohibition on films on circuit.....
See Someswar Bhowmik, *Cinema and Censorship: The Politics of Control in India* (New Delhi: Orient Blackswan, 2009: 31).

WRITING AND ARCHIVING THE SELF: CONVERSATIONS AND BIOGRAPHIES | 1

A SHORT NOTE ON *DEVDAS*

D*evdas* (Dir. Pramathesh Barua, 1935) is an adaptation of Sarat Chandra Chattopadhyay's canonical Bengali novella *Devdas* (1917). The editorial of *Chitra* (9 October-November 1935), the publicity journal of New Theatres Ltd., described the film as 'a purely psychological effect...and Barua is a master of film psychology. He thinks, he feels, he lives his sequences before he accepts them....' Advertised as 'a story of broken hearts' (in a publicity flyer, 1935), Barua's *Devdas* is a tragic love story between young Devdas (Dev da) and Parvati (Paro). After growing up together, Devdas eventually rebuts Parvati's advances since he is uncertain about his feelings towards her. Later, out of despair, Parvati accepts the proposal of an elderly widower, only to realize that she and Devdas are deeply in love. The epic component of the plot develops as Devdas goes away from the village to the city (and later to endless distressing travels) and meets the courtesan Chadramukhi. He in time takes to drinking and returns to die at Parvati's doorstep. Devdas's journey from the village to the city and desperate attempts to retreat to the village and to his own past, exemplifies the apprehensions regarding the degeneration of the village, and the angst of the migrant zamindars (landed gentry) and bhadraloks. Indeed, Devdas performs the bleakness of the larger history and social transformation, and becomes an archetypal character who moves away from an archetypal village to an archetypal city.

When Barua transformed the plot of Chattopadhyay's novella, the film as well as the iconic melancholic character of Devdas recreated its own range of meanings. Moreover, Barua introduced several changes. For instance, during the sequence of Devdas's 'last journey' in the film, the sky turns black and the leaves turn white as he gets closer to Paro and to his death. Barua had used a special coloured filter to get this dark and ominous 'wash' effect introduced by the Bengal School of Art. Furthermore, in the elaborate last sequence, the door becomes an index of Paro's entrapment as Barua inter-cuts shots of Paro running through the vast mansion, with shots of the huge door gradually shutting her in. The last shot of the film—the burning pyre and the blind seer (K. C. Dey) singing the song about death ('*Teri maut...*'/Your Death...') made an influential visual impact to be used in other films. This departure from the ending in the novella, where the narrator attempts to arouse pity for the deceased person, appears to be a permanent departure to which later directors insistently return, while the image of Paro running towards Devdas comes back in other films. In addition, the point that 'virtually a generation wept over Barua's *Devdas*' is crucial.[1] In fact, it is rather curious that the singing star of Barua's *Devdas*, K. L. Saigal, also suffered from Devdas's alcoholism and died at the age of 42. Along similar lines, the author of the novella, Sarat Chandra Chattopadhyay, who had travelled from the village to the city, is remembered for his unruly lifestyle. In addition, Barua himself remarked in 1951:

> '*Devdas* was in me even before I was born, I created it every moment of my life much before I put it on screen and yet, once it was on the screen, it was more than a mirage, a play of light and shade and sadder still, it ceased to exist after two hours.'[2]

It is clearly uncanny that so many biographies merged into this one narrative and character, raising questions regarding the apprehensions concerning modernity, which produced nearly a 'pathological' identification with the film and the character. Certainly, the image of Barua's '*Devdas*' is an enduring one, which gets disseminated beyond the film, and Barua's film becomes an archetype.[3]

ON JAMUNA BARUA

Jamuna Barua (also Jumna and Jumuna Devi) was well-known actor from the 1930s. She shot to fame with the legendary film *Devdas* (1935). While she played 'Paro' in the film, Jamuna spent her life with the celebrated actor-director Pramathesh Barua (also P.C. Barua). Her career took off in the thirties with a short role in *Mohabbat Ki Kasauti* (Dir.P.C. Barua, 1934). As narrated by Kananbala (also Kanan Devi) in her biography (translated here), after she was unable to play the part, Jamuna was called from Barua's residence (see Jamuna Barua's interview) and she eventually became the enigmatic Paro of the film.

Jamuna Barua in Sesh Uttar

Writing about Barua's *Devdas,* K.A. Abbas remarked, 'Do you remember it? Out of the very lens of the camera walked away the slender figure of a woman, going further and further... .'[4] Indeed, she had an enigmatic quality about her, and especially her shrouded personal life created a series of myths around her. Her brief, yet, illuminating interview, anthologized here, highlights the ways in which young and vulnerable (female) actors were employed in the industry and how historical narratives have rarely tackled their significance.

Jamuna Barua continued to act in Barua's films like *Grihadaha* (1936), *Maya* (1936), *Adhikar* (1939), *Uttarayan* (1941), *Sesh Uttar* (1942), *Chander Kalanka* (1944), though she rarely worked with other directors (see interview). She also acted in a series of Hindi films like *Amiree, Pehchan* and *Iran Ki Ek Raat* directed by Barua. She worked with few other directors and did Bengali films like *Debar* (1943), *Nilanguriya* (1943) and *Malancha* (1953). Jamuna Barua was well known for her stoic presence, her slim figure and a longish face that fitted well with the 'Rabindrik' prototype. She played the quintessential bhadromahila in some of Barua films, and her role in *Adhikar* and *Sesh Uttar*, in which she is pitted against the beautiful and charming singer-actor Kananbala, were crucial moments of her career.[5]

CONVERSATIONS ON *DEVDAS* WITH JAMUNA BARUA

Madhuja Mukherjee (MM): Tell me about *Devdas* (1935), about its making and your involvement in it.[6]

Jamuna Barua (JB): I was about 14 then. He [Barua] needed a very young girl to act in his upcoming production.[7] I used to live in his home. He asked me to act in his new film. In fact, he had initially wanted to make *Charitraheen* [the iconic novel by Sarat Chandra Chattopadhyay on the Bengali babu's life in the city],[8] however, he made *Devdas* eventually. We shot at New Theatres II (studios).[9] He gave [cameraperson and director] Nitin Bose's assistant [at that time], Bimal Roy, an opportunity to shoot the film.[10] But he used to dictate the shots; Bimal was trained through the process of making of *Devdas*. After the film, Bimal was ready.[11] He [Barua] also fostered Pankaj Mullick [well-known singer and music composer] personally.[12] He gave all members associated with the production a chance to prove themselves, though no one writes about him any more.

MM: Can you describe the last scene of *Devdas*? It is clearly not treated in the same manner in the novel. While in the novel Parvati gets to know about Devdas' death only in the next morning, in the film she runs through corridors to catch that last glimpse of the dying man, which is harshly denied to her.

JB: Yes, in the last scene, Parvati runs towards Devdas, crying his name aloud, 'Devdas, Devdas…'. He sympathized with the plight of women at that time, with young girls being married off early and made to succumb to so many restrictions! Now, I suppose, things have changed, you can marry the man of your choice. He [Barua] wanted to show that our society refuses to understand women.[13] Sarat Chandra [Chattopadhyay] had later [after the release of the film] remarked, 'You [Barua] have done something that I could not do'. But I do not remember much [about the making of the film], I did not socialize much. It was he who guided me.[14]

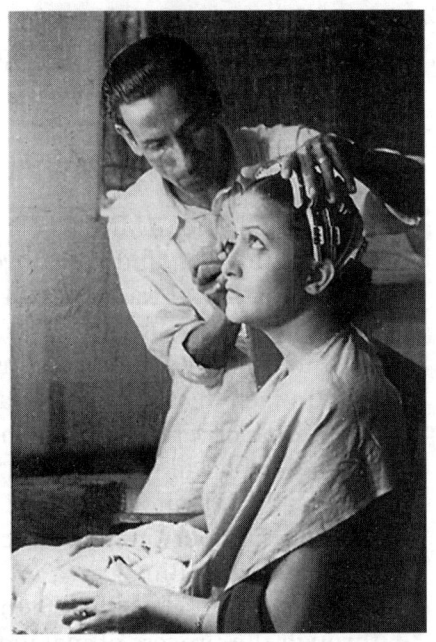

Jamuna Barua getting prepared for a shoot

MM: Generally speaking, how did the shooting take place? Did Barua discuss the screenplay with you?

JB: We used to rehearse a lot. For *Devdas*, we shot outdoors with reflectors. We did not have artificial lights back then, he got it much later from abroad, at the time he had visited England.[15] But actors, by and large, were never consulted.[16] Neither did we discuss the script. Perhaps experienced artists could decide to act by themselves, but we [the junior artists] could not, we were still learning. We, however, got the script beforehand and had [training] classes during which we would rehearse for days; it was the way in which actors practise in theatres. We had a fixed schedule. It was like this in New Theatres, however, I am not much aware about other production houses. I have rarely acted in films other than the ones he had made.

MM: Can you explain in detail about the day-to-day shooting procedure?

JB: We did not have the playback system at that point of time. The orchestra was placed on the floor. They would sit there [on the shooting floor] and the artist would look at their movements and perform.[17] Technically things have improved in present times. For make-up, we used some powder and at times some *alta* [red paint] on the face and neck. Later, actors generally used Max Factor [cosmetics] products. It is different now, even unattractive girls look beautiful with make-up! *Devdas*, I remember, had very simple costume.[18]

MM: What about the studio structure? How did it function?

JB: B. N. Sircar [the visionary proprietor of New Theatres] never spoke to the women folk.[19] He would only speak to the directors. They [directors] would choose the story and then decide upon the sets, costumes and acting style. Acting was generally rather poor at that time! He [Barua] introduced natural acting. But New Theatres was a very big production house. It had a huge staff, hired too many artists, and there were too many people with too many opinions. In fact, the cost of production was higher than the profits. The Bombay stars always got more than us. They would get as much as Rs7000 per month, while someone like Uma Sashi [of *Chandidas* fame][20] and us would receive about a thousand.[21] Now [since post-independence], there is one picture contract.[22] As a matter of fact, Bombay had a much bigger market, so the films earned a larger profit. But he [Barua] never had any plans for Bombay.

MM: Why didn't Barua go to Bombay, while others shifted at the point when the studio system was disintegrating?[23]

JB: The students [young, educated, college-going beginners] loved him a lot. They idolized him. He was very popular amongst them. Once they came up to him and requested him not to shift to Bombay. He agreed and kept his promise. Even when he disagreed with Sircar Saheb [B.N. Sircar], he did not relocate to Bombay. He was, moreover, sceptical about making films in Hindi and about his own fluency in the language. I used to receive many fan letters at that time, and producers [like Ranjit Studios and Pancholi Arts] in Bombay wanted to cast me in their productions. But he never appreciated the idea. Since he never went to Bombay, I too stayed back. He used to say, 'You will not be able to manage by yourself.'

ON KANANBALA

Kananbala (aka Kanan Devi) began her career with the Madan Theatres during the silent era and performed in about five films (between 1926 and 1932) with them, belonging to disparate genres and characters, which apparently included male characters as well.[24] However, her career took off with Radha Films (during 1933–36), thereafter with New Theatres (during 1937–41), and later with MP Productions (1942–48). While with New Theatres she did a series of outstanding films, her popularity as a singer soared with her renditions of Rabindrasangeet in *Mukti* (1937), soulful *bhajans* in *Vidyapati* (1938) and several popular numbers performed in *Street Singer* (Dir. Phani Mazumdar, 1938), *Sapera* (Dir. Debaki Bose, 1939), *Jawani Ki Reet* (Dir. Hemchandra Chunder, 1939), *Parajay* (Dir. Hemchandra Chunder, 1940), *Abhinetri* (Dir. Amar Mallik, 1940), *Lagan* (Dir. Nitin Bose, 1941), *Parichay* (Dir. Nitin Bose, 1941), and so on.

Her popularity was mythical and may be compared only with Devika Rani, a star of the Bombay Talkies. For instance, Raghunath Kundu in his fan poem titled 'Our Trio' (in *Chitrapanji*, 1938, September) describes the ethereal beauty of the actress and mentions the ways by which Kananbala 'gleans the nectar of spring (flowers)'. Her singing abilities initiated a number of films where she enacted the singer (and was often paired with legendary singer K.L. Saigal).

She was initially trained under Ustad Allah Rakha and cut a series of discs for the Megaphone Gramophone Company. More important, nevertheless, is the setting up of her own production company, namely, Shrimati Pictures, which clearly show the significance of her abilities, as well the ways in which women actors contributed to the film industry. Sections of her biography translated here, underscore a range of her own uncertainties (as well the anguish young entrants suffer). It demonstrates in great detail the day-to-day functioning within the studios, and brings to light various nuances of filmmaking as well as the import of the (female) actors in the entire industrial process. Her excessive flowery style and yet, a deliberate restraint in tackling the content, bring forth the strains through which women write culture.

I SALUTE ALL: KANAN DEVI

The news of my joining New Theatres, after leaving Radha Films, had spread across the film industry around April or May 1936.[25] Though I desired to leave earlier, I was late in parting with Radha Films.[26] I remember that [director-actor] Pramathesh Barua had offered me the role of Parvati in *Devdas*. Since I had already entered into a contract with Radha Films, I missed this exceptional opportunity. I was extremely upset at the play of destiny, depriving me of such a golden chance. New Theatres was the most sophisticated organization in those days. In tinsel town, Mr. Barua was like a fairytale hero

Kananbala in Bishabriksha, *a Radha Films Productions*

in our times. Working with him and under his direction was like achieving the impossible. Sarat Chandra's [Chattopadhyay's] novel was another incentive for me. I got this rare opportunity without any effort, but unfortunately, I could not respond—I felt it was my fate in action. Later, I came to know that the hurdles were not genuine, they had emerged mainly due to the negligence of the authorities of Radha Films, and it was a way of harassing the inexperienced and the vulnerable actors.

Kanan Devi in Mukti, *a New Theatres Production*

I felt helpless and was completely shattered with the rejection. To help me regain my mental strength, my mother had arranged for my initiation into the religious order [*diksha*]. When a person becomes helpless, he/she treads into dark alleys sans all directions in life, and questions the existence of God. It is in such moments of crisis that one obtains spiritual strength suddenly and unexpectedly, which provides assurance of God's existence. I soon realized that this was the means of finding a new direction...

The usual course of my life changed [after diksha]. I realized that in this mundane world there is a form. If one gets to know that form, the mind will immediately be contented. There is a Call, to which the mind responds; there is the Light that the mind perceives.

This is a rare moment. It comes once, but when it comes, it changes one's entire perspective of life. I nurtured the moment in my mind, in the form of a seedling, which later attained the form of a huge tree. I shall explain this experience later.

Soon thereafter, my career at the New Theatres began. The day I first went to the floor of New Theatres, I was very excited and I can never forget the day. ...But the excitement and interest with which I went turned out to be a big disappointment on the very first day.

Since the afternoon, I waited at the studio. There was no one to talk to, none to brief me about my role. Everyone, beginning with the attendants to the senior personnel, had a stoic and snobbish disposition. 'We are not ordinary, we work under the New Theatres' banner'—was what they seemed to think about themselves, and this was evident in their behaviour. The afternoon rolled over to dusk and dusk gave way to evening. Suddenly, everyone was jolted into action. 'What is the matter?' I asked. I heard, 'Sahib is arriving.' Sahib? I looked surprised. Pitying my ignorance an attendant approached me and said, 'Sahib is B. N. Sircar—the God of New Theatres! And, you should remember this.' Soon, adjusting his belt and cap, and putting up a modest and saintly look on his face, the man rushed towards the sahib's car. ...People dressed in suits, tightened the knots of their tie and wiped their faces with handkerchiefs. Few straightened their shirt collars. Others in dhoti-kurta, straightened the curves on their sleeves and holding the folds of the dhoti in their hands, as if approaching the playground, rushed towards greeting B. N. Sircar as his car approached. This was followed by the desperate scramble to draw their sahib's attention first, then greeting him to express their loyalty to the master. Sitting and waiting through the day had made me tired and frustrated; however, I became inquisitive about the affairs around. Unknowingly, I had got up and had started approaching the scene. Suddenly I halted and observed how the sycophants, though well established and experienced, behaved immaturely, shoving at each other and trying to open the door of their sahib's car. After almost all of them had prostrated before him on the ground to greet him, they followed him as soon as Sircar stepped out of the car and started walking. I was surprised that nobody felt it necessary to introduce me to him though I was an artist who belonged to the same production house, had joined my duty on that very day, and had been waiting for the entire day. Everyone was preoccupied with themselves. Who had the time to look after someone as petty as me? The experience was astonishing as well as sad! However, from some distance I managed to greet him with a namaskar and came back to another room. I did not know if my greetings had caught Sir B.N. Sircar's attention in that crowd but I thought that being an artist of his organization, it would be discourteous on my part not to acknowledge him on the first day of my work. Or else, this would trouble me in future. Sitting for another two hours, I asked Mr. P. N. Roy [a senior executive at New Theatres], 'May I leave now?' He was surprised to see me and commented, 'You are still sitting?' I felt thoroughly dejected.

There is something I must mention in this context. The narrative of my first day's experience at New Theatres was in no way aimed at humiliating or mocking Sir B.N. Sircar. One would grossly misinterpret my intention, if read from such a perspective. What I wanted to bring to light was the atmosphere at New Theatres and not comment on him.

I must mention here with all modesty that my first glance of Sir B.N. Sircar left a deep impact in my mind. Addressed as 'Sahib', he truly appeared being one. He spoke less and his serious disposition reflected his sophistication and courteous nature, which made his personality all the more attractive. I do not think the false flattery around him had any impact on his mind. He had the regal presence of an emperor seated in his kingdom. None could hear an extra word from him other than those related to work.

We [female actors] did not get the chance to speak to him directly. Going by the norms of the place, our requirements, grievances and opinions would reach him via another person. I do not know whether he was informed regarding everything. But any request that reached his ears was definitely looked into. The festival number of *Amrita Bazar* [newspaper] carried an article stating Sircar Sahib's comment on his unawareness about the artists involved in his production. In this regard, the grievances of the artists (I am stating particularly my opinion) were deeply entrenched. But I considered such a response from the artists as being natural as we hardly got an opportunity to meet or interact with him. Why did Mr. Sircar not initiate a custom of holding direct meetings and discussions with him and make arrangements to share important information with him? Later whenever I got the chance to speak to him or discuss little issues with him, I looked up to him with great respect as he spoke in his compassionate, broadminded and affectionate manner. I would, in fact, repent why I did not get such an opportunity earlier. Perhaps then I could have worked with more ease and felt more contented! I realized that he was a spontaneous connoisseur of art and artists. He had greatly helped in the advancement of the Indian film industry by bringing under his banner renowned artists, music directors, lyricists and directors. Bengalis should be indebted to him for his contribution. In the world of entertainment, the respect and admiration that the Indian film industry acquired would have remained a distant dream if entrepreneurs like B. N. Sircar had not steered it to success through several unfavourable conditions. At that time, the social elite despised cinema and theatre. But Sircar, who belonged to an aristocratic family, left his domain of skills and his profession [of civil engineering], and joined a business to perfect an art form that was in those days considered to be ridiculous (films then had not achieved the status of a distinct art form).[27] This required great courage, something which is hard to think of now. I take this opportunity to salute this determined and successful man because of whom we have earned so much respect!

The experience of the first day at New Theatres made me very depressed. How would I work here? Everyone at New Theatres was extremely selfish and preoccupied with themselves. Where would I go? How would I work? What would be the disposition of the people directing me? Such a snobbish environment would perhaps affect others too. Probably they would look down upon us and find fault at every step. Probably due to my naivety, I would become a laughing stock before them. Would I be able to work with self-respect? Everything was dark before my eyes. I felt like a village damsel being lost in the glitz and glamour of the urban setting.[28]

'KANANBALA IN VIDYAPATI'

My first film under the New Theatres banner was *Vidyapati* (though the first film released in theatres was *Mukti*). In *Vidyapati*, my role as Anuradha was a landmark not only in my career as an artist but also in my personal life. Here I am referring to the experiences I have had so far, until then I had worked only to meet my daily material needs. In such circumstances, sustenance was the primary objective, nurturing of bigger dreams fetched merely momentary pleasure. Anuradha's laughter, tears, sorrow, love and restraint, however, provided me with a scope to vent out my pent-up emotions. By enacting her character, my reality and my desires got a common platform of expression

Kananbala as the enigmatic Anuradha

Kananbala and Cchaya Devi in intense scenes in Vidyapati

and I got to know myself in a new way, which I had not expected. *Vidyapati* was also made in Hindi and my work was recognized and acclaimed by the film connoisseurs of Indian cinema. While *Manmayee Girl's School* helped me to establish myself as an actor, *Vidyapati* earned me a pan-India reputation. *Vidyapati*'s Anuradha brought an astonishing period of change in my life.[29]

I owe my success to Debaki Bose [director],[30] and Raichand Boral [music director].[31] For an artist to mature, it is important that he/she is guided and supported by a capable mentor who shows him/her the right learning method. For me, Debaki Bose, hence, was indispensable. With affection, discipline and appreciation, and occasional criticisms, he had mastered the art of making people work and at the same time be responsible for their performance. He made me aware of the different dimensions to be taken into account while portraying Anuradha's character. He guided me where I was needed to emphasize on Anuradha's expression of unbounded affection for others, where I was required to under act and show restraint, and how to present the latent strains of remorse that lay hidden behind her apparent contented nature. He carved out with perfection the desired finesse in performance. It cannot be denied that it was only possible for me to carry out such a difficult task with ease since I got a teacher like him.

If acting and singing were to be compared as two dimensions of Anuradha's character, the latter instilled in her a certain degree of liveliness. The *padavali*, in a curious combination of Maithili and Bengali, brought out poetic nuances, expressing a rainbow of emotions through a mix of tears and smiles. Its wonderful combination of rhythm and lyrics thoroughly engrossed me. Since I would be totally absorbed in singing, I felt a sense of oneness with the character. All the songs in *Vidyapati* are melodious, however, '*Angneme auob jab rasiya*' led me to the helm of fame. A particular gramaphone company has included this number in my Hindi long-playing disc, and I am truly obliged to them. The success of this song and the fame it brought to me is largely due to Raichandbabu. I shall come to this later. I should mention Durgadas Bandyopadhyay [of *Chandidas* fame], who although was not the hero of this film was almost its protagonist.[32] The visualization of Anuradha in *Vidyapati* was Kazi Sahib's [Kazi Nazrul Islam] contribution.[33]

Durgababu was, as can be described, an epic hero. Sanskrit epithets describing heroes as 'broad chest; arms as long as a *sal* tree; wide forehead; large eyes; complexion as radiant as gold', and so on, befitted him. Such a handsome man is rarely to be found. He was a blissfully happy person. Whenever I remember Durgababu, I am reminded of his uninhibited loud laughter. One could easily gauge how nice an individual he was from his smile. In the beginning, I was very nervous to work with such a powerful actor. He was not only elder to me, he was a more experienced actor. While I

The teasing smiles of Anuradha: Kananbala with Amar Mullick

had just earned a bit of success in my career, he was already midway in his career, and at the height of fame.

I remember the dilemma I underwent during the shoot. I could sing a song with him but was not comfortable enacting gestures like stealing a glance, or looking at him teasingly. Understanding my uneasiness, Durgababu, one day, suddenly rushed towards me and holding my shoulders with his hands said, '*Jowarer jal*' [an expression used in the film, meaning water of high-tide], look at me!' I looked at him shyly, a bit cowered, but he in his usual manner laughed loudly enlivening the entire studio. I started laughing too overcoming my initial inhibitions. In a moment, he seemed to be so close to me. I have already mentioned earlier that our whereabouts at the studio and time of arrival and departure were strictly monitored at the studio. After having worked with him for another day, on our next meeting he patted my shoulders and said warmly, 'Come and sit here.' These words brought tears to my eyes unknowingly. He was sympathetic towards all big and small artists, and workers in the studio. Durgababu, an openhearted extrovert, was a great artist but was also impulsive.

I remember, one day, we had to stop shooting for some reason. But Durgababu was desperate to carry on the shooting. Why will we not shoot? Nobody could explain to him. I approached him and said, 'Dada [brother] carrying on the shooting is really not possible today.' These words brought a sudden change in his temperament. 'When my Didi [sister] is saying, then it must not be really possible', and saying this, he patted my back and left with a laughter that echoed through the entire studio.

Durgababu's mannerisms were very theatrical. It complemented well with his physical characteristics. The word 'majestic' is truly apt for him. I heard that he had occupied a berth forcefully without reservations in some train, and during the course of disagreement he told the then minister, Fazlul Haq, 'If Fazlul Haq dies, a second will be re-born but if

Durga Barrujje [Durgadas Bandyopadhyay] dies there will be no second.' This comment though reflects on his theatrically charged egoistic self, it suited one of Durgababu's stature. There has been no second Durga Bandyopadhyay yet.

The songs of *Vidyapati*, which gave me monumental fame overnight, owed its indebtedness to music director Raichand Boral. From the padavali, Debakibabu had made a judicious choice of the most beautiful songs. Raibabu rendered those songs with a melodious life force. How he taught us to perfection extracting the exact *natyarasa* is only known to us who have been his co-workers. Raibabu would repeatedly remind us that a film song should never be treated just as a song. Every moment it should be remembered that the song is a dialogue; a part of the narrative of the film. Modulated according to the mood, the tunes and melodies would be influenced by the situation in which the song would be placed. I remember how he changed a *mir* [musical ornamentation] several times. He would not spare anyone not even himself till he felt that the message the character wanted to convey matched the rhythm of the tune.[34] The Maithili pronunciations in *Vidyapati* were emphasized by Raibabu [since Maithili was the original language in which Vidyapati's padavalis/ poems were written] and before teaching us the songs, he would make us recite the verses and like a strict examiner check each pronunciation individually. He would keep strict vigilance over the fact that words and tunes were equally accentuated. He felt that the melody could not be monotonous in the *sthayi* [core musical structure of a raga] and the *antara* [variations of the sthayi on a higher scale]. The songs had to match the pace of the narrative in the film. If it was a climax scene, the song would begin from a high pitch. If a song sequence had to be placed where the characters were self-absorbed in thought then the song would start silently without any kind of orchestration. According to Debakibabu's instructions, language, sentiments, tunes—all were based on *Vaishnava rasas*.[35]

As an example, the song '*Angneme auob jab rasiya*' was a mixture of *hasya* [comic] and *madhura* [sweet] rasa. It was used as a dialogue with actor Amar Mullick.[36] As in a dialogue, the element of drama was essential to be emphasized. Hence, restrain and fast rhythmic pace were used to emphasize on the undertone of mockery. In the last verse, the pitch was supposed to rise quite high, and then after a halt, drop to a lower scale. Raibabu had taught these finer nuances with such care! At the time of recording, Raibabu would stand with his hands raised. His hand and eye movements were enough to express his level of satisfaction with our rendition of the song. What anxious moments we had! When he was satisfied with our performances, his eyes would brighten up and that was enough to indicate that we had passed the test. How elated we would be! I realize now how contented we were when we worked; there were so many exciting and enriching experiences. I doubt if artists in present times have a life so fulfilling!

In contemporary times, the 'music take' is done in a different place with a successful playback singer, while the actual shooting takes place in some other place.[37] There has been such unimaginable technical progress, which has made everyone's work easier and has minimized possibilities of errors. From different places, bits and pieces of finished products are assembled and the machine-made product is made ready instantly. [Earlier], the work of the established director, technician, artist or make-up persons as a combined whole through experimentation, thoughts, training, anxieties, dedication led to a natural result of gratification. In the films of yesteryears there would be many faults. Some would be due to lack of technical facilities or of experience. But all flaws in the film were overshadowed by the spontaneity in each worker. It is because of this reason that the films of the yesteryears still entertain today's audiences. I remember that the same [theme] music was played right from the credit title of *Vidyapati* to the first scene, sometimes emphasizing on the subject or at times describing the *vasant utsav* [spring festival]. Besides this, there used to be so many variations of the melody [in other scenes]. Raibabu was experienced in working with the orchestra, and therefore, this experience helped him in experimenting with the ups and downs and harmonization of tunes. The 'take' took us only 12 minutes, as far as I can recall. Raibabu warned us saying, 'Just before the "take", you will get four chances. Not more than that.' However, we did not need that. We finished in two shots. We had rehearsed for around two hundred times. I can still visualize the 'take'; it was taken in the open air (not inside any studio). B. N. Sircar, Pramathesh Barua and P. N. Roy—all the stalwarts of the New Theatres—were waiting with great interest. There was a huge crowd outside [the studio]. It was a great test ahead as well as an occasion to rejoice. Did the audience love *Vidyapati*'s Anuradha because she added life to the film?

I have already mentioned before that though *Vidyapati* was made earlier, my first released film under the banner of New Theatres was *Mukti* (17 September 1937). *Vidyapati* was released much later than *Mukti* on 22 April 1938. Outside Kolkata, in Bombay and Karachi, the film was first shown in the first week of December 1938, that is, three months after *Mukti* was released in Hindi.

Before I mention anything about *Mukti* and Pramathesh Barua, I want to state something very personal and dear to my heart.

Today I am recognized as an established actor. To me, the most coveted possession is my songs. The audiences are acquainted with my songs only as much as they have heard the numbers in the films. I established contact with the divine via music. My life diverged in various kinds of work, sought refuge in music, which I found truly rejuvenating. Whenever I would listen to a song, I would be hypnotized. I would gain back my senses when I would hear the call of my elder sister, either to take a bath or have lunch. The few songs Bholada[38] taught me affectionately were my only possession. At leisure, I would hum those songs to myself. My feelings were similar to a poor person who whenever she got some time would bring out her long cherished savings and would see them privately and be contented about it. Like an untutored apprentice, I would feel very happy while singing those songs.

While working in Madan Theatres,[39] I had some money and started learning music from [the eminent exponent of classical Indian music] Ustad Allah Rakha. As far as I can remember, he was from Lucknow and was very affectionate towards me. He used to teach me the *sargam* [structure of musical scales] with great care. He advised me to continue with the *riyaaz* [practice] every day early morning with a light wrapper around the throat. The hours of riyaaz as advised by him were at first fifteen minutes, then half an hour, which later was raised to two hours. He would always encourage me with words like, '*Beti* [daughter], carry on your riyaaz. The world of Hindustani [classical] music will pay its respect to you and you will also become famous. Great people will honour you.' I would become so happy imagining myself at the pinnacle of fame. I would learn one raga after the other and imagine approaching my destination as the locked doors were opening one after the other before me.

He taught me a song based on raga Yaman, an evening-time raga. The lyrics probably went as: '*sab gunijan yaman gao*'. But I must admit that I had not liked the raga then. I started liking it much later. In the prime years of life, when I had almost done away with my training as a singer, every time I listened to the raga I would feel nostalgic. But that was much later. When I first started training in this raga, I felt that it lacked any rasa [emotions]. Ustad understood my feelings and changed Yaman to Purbi. The melancholic notes of Purbi touched my soul. Whenever I would sing Purbi, I could visualize the words, as if the raga heralded the onset of the darkness of night and in the fading light of the day a melancholic sky was created. In that vanishing light I could visualize an ascetic walking and singing to himself. Is the tune of wanderlust reflected in raga Purbi? In the morning, whenever I listened to Bhairabi, I dedicated myself to the feet of Bhairab [Lord Shiva]. There was a tone of gloom in raga Bhairo, but the remorse was of a different nature, devoid of the reclusiveness of Purbi. It inspired life to bloom. When teaching Bhairo, Ustad used to caution me that if the mind is not kept free, death would follow. Thereafter, when rendering this raga I often would find myself detached from the listeners, lost in the melody, and found profound joy, something, which I had not experienced earlier.

I did not learn to sing the ragas meant to be sung at nighttime. I learnt Behag, a raga closest to my heart. The sorrow of separation of an estranged beauty from her lover forms the essence of this raga. But the expression of her feelings is detrimental to her dignity. In that raga, I felt as if a wall of solemnity built a barrier around such a sense of estrangement. Ustad used to say with a smile, 'My girl, if you practice this raga you will master it. This raga matches completely with your persona.' In order to achieve mastery over a raga one needs to be fortunate. I failed to achieve it; perhaps I was not born with that fortune.

I could not do the riyaaz with the dedication that Ustad asked for. There was intense work pressure at the studios. Saddened, Ustad decided to leave one day. Before he left, Ustad poignantly told me, 'One day you will know what you have lost in your quest for fame and money. Even after much riyaaz many do not get the voice that God has given you. You disrespected such a gift just for popularity. A time will come when you will get to the fact that there is nothing of your own. You will surely regret that day.'

Now, I am not as busy as I used to be. Even when I have retracted from the world outside, how much time do I really have to sit back and introspect? On certain days and on sleepless nights I take a stroll in the garden. The blooming fullness of the chrysanthemum makes me realize

that I have achieved many things, which I never desired, nor do I think I deserve them. God has blessed me in many ways. Yet there remains a huge void, which cannot be filled. Life seems to get out of hand owing to my various activities during the day. Evening brings back order. The dense darkness of the night intensifies the mystery of life. Then, from every corner, remorseful questions arise and demand answers. I can hear their muted language, but cannot answer them. I myself have not been able to find answers to these questions.

If I do not mention about Kazi Sahib, the *Vidyapati* episode remains incomplete. As stated earlier, in *Vidyapati*, Anuradha's character had been visualized by Kazi Sahib himself.

Probably, long before working in *Vidyapati*, J. N. Ghosh [of New Theatres] introduced me to [the maverick poet and composer] Nazrul [Kazi Nazrul Islam] in the rehearsal room of Megaphone [gramophone company]. Before this meeting, I knew him as a public figure. That day, I was formally introduced to him for the first time. I was afraid to look at the famous poet. I was just an ordinary girl. But I soon realized that there was nothing to fear. He was in a kurta with a mass of long hair, curling down till his neck. He was playing the harmonium with eyes closed and was humming a tune. At times, he would look up with his eyes and stare elsewhere, distracted, but it was evident that he was thinking about something else. After he stopped playing the harmonium, he looked at me. His eyes were large and had a glow. He read my hesitation instantly. To make me feel easy, he praised my songs, my voice and my looks while the entire room reverberated with light-hearted mirth. My hesitation vanished in a moment. Looking at J. N. Ghosh, Nazrul said 'I am feeling hungry; Kanan's face shows that she is hungry too. Brother, please take note of this', and others soon broke out in a roll of laughter. J. N. Ghosh immediately became and arranged for food and sweets, as well as a plate of

leaves and aromatic tobacco. As soon as the food arrived, Nazrul gave me a handful of ten to twelve sweets and finished the rest in a moment. As a person, Nazrul was very cheerful and a hearty eater as well. But then, he could spend hours absorbed in music, forgetting to sleep or eat. What a surprising way of being self-absorbed! If any tune struck his chords, he would immediately try to fill in the words. At times, lyrics would demand tunes. I may not have deep knowledge on the ragas and raginis, but I could not overlook the emotional intensity with which he would go on searching the tunes in a harmonium. It seemed that he tried to find out the real meaning of a raga by finding the right lyrics.

Observing my surprised expressions, once, he said, 'What are you looking at with your wide eyes? I am a *ghatak* [matchmaker], do you know that? In one country resides the tunes and in another the words. The bride and groom from two different countries need to be united. But if the castes of the two become different, it would be a mismatch. Do you understand anything?' Then with a smile, he looked at me. I shook my head in denial and said, 'No, I did not understand.' He answered, 'You will understand later.' I do not know whether I did understand or not but later I had an incomprehensive feeling about the poet. If it was easy to get to know the poet in him through his works, it was equally difficult to get hold of his personality who would play around with words for tunes, and with tunes for words, filling in each with infinite qualities.

With regard to *Vidyapati*, I am reminded about yet another co-artist—Pahari Sanyal.[40] I have observed that he has remained the same throughout his career—always spontaneous, lively and zestful. He would inspire everyone and complement all in superlatives. He would always suit the role of a handsome, wide-hearted and imaginative hero. Paharibabu played the title role in *Vidyapati*. His pleasant, sweet smile still retains its youthfulness and has remained the same over the years.

After *Vidyapati*, it was time to work for *Mukti*. The feeling of adventure associated with it was never to be forgotten. I had missed an opportunity to work in Mr. Barua's film as Parvati [in *Devdas*]. At last, I had got the golden opportunity of working with him without much effort of mine. I remembered the voice of my gurudev, reading out the Bhagavad, '*Parjay jogadvihitang bidhatra kalen sarbang labhate manushya*'—everything has been kept for a person in succession. We get it on time. Unnecessary hullabaloo is not beneficial. The thing I had desired and for which I had repented once had come to me.

When Mr. Barua contacted me for the role of Parvati in *Devdas*,...I was in a contract with Radha films and so could not take up his offer. ...Vishnupriya of *Srigouranga*, Niharika of *Manmayee Girl's School* had brought fame and name for me. So I was always eager to maintain a cordial relationship free of any misunderstandings with them. ...[When] I met Mr. Barua for the first time...[he] was at that point of time, quite famous and very popular...But deep in my heart, the gorgeous, dream-like images I had of him did not match the real Barua. Thin and short, his eyes reflected his self-confidence...since I could not enact the role of Parvati, I was quite depressed. ... Mr. Barua reassured me, '...There is nothing to be sad about. I think in future we will get such opportunities.' ...Opportunities did come in future. During the shooting of *Mukti* I saw him in his workplace for the first time. I had been keen on working with him, but my experience was not as exciting [on the first day]. On the first day, I could not even meet him.

Next day I arrived ten minutes before my schedule. I met Mr. Barua but the glorious image I had in mind about his procedure of work did not match with the situation. He explained the character of *Chitra* in a few words. But I was not contented. I stumbled for the second time.

I must explain things at this point. He was a contemporary director at this time. I had expected that a director of his stature would train us in his own techniques through rehearsals on acting skills in order to bring out the soul of the character. I expected he would show us how to transport tension in scenes and explain such rudimentary aspects. But I was not so fortunate. Next day Mr. Barua instructed his assistant to narrate the story to me. Subsequently, the assistant narrated the story of *Mukti* in short. I felt very helpless. The people I have worked with previously have explained things elaborately—the ways of acting, feelings to be evoked, emotions of the character, as well as the reactions. But Mr. Barua left everything on me. He just stated that 'Chitra's character has a fascinating contradiction within her. On the one hand, were society and public shows and the arrogance to display the glorious moments of joy and fortune before others, on the other hand, was her unbounded attraction towards Prasanta's unexpressed love.' Everyone understood him, but somewhere I was hesitant. I was young. I was slowly becoming popular. While acting opposite someone as experienced as Pramatheshbabu, I used to feel very restricted. Added to that was the fact that my acting and expression of emotions did not invoke any reaction from him. I read this as indifference on his part. At certain places, I would feel that I was missing by just a little. Some suggestions at those junctures would have been extremely helpful. But I did not receive any such help. As I was young, I felt he did not want my talents to blossom in full. Though several issues went on in my mind, I could not express my difficulties due to many reasons. First, unlike now, it was not a heroine-dominated industry. The heroines did not have the discretion either to select or reject roles according to their choice. The director's words were like the Bible to be followed. During those times, the practice of script reading was also not prevalent. The little needed for enacting the role was narrated, nothing more was ever mentioned. Besides, Mr. Barua was very popular in those days. His words in the industry were as important as divine dictates. Others would be referred as 'babu' but

Kananbala as the modern woman in Mukti

being a *rajkumar* [since he was the prince of Gauripur, Assam] nobody could dare to call Mr. Barua 'Pramatheshbabu'. He would be referred to as 'Barua Sahib'. Complaints could be made to babus, but it was beyond imagination to do so to a sahib.

However, because of this, personally I had gained a lot. Earlier I was dependant on the directors. This was the first time I worked on my own and started to rely on my own abilities. This self-confidence was indirectly an endowment from Mr. Barua. I consider myself indebted to him. *Mukti* was loved by all (I have heard that *Mukti* will be re-released again. This is definitely a mark of the film's popularity beyond a single generation). Yet, I felt that I could not act freely in this film. It was probably because of the songs that *Mukti* became popular. Certainly, this was my guess and might not be correct completely.

Much later, I worked with Mr. Barua in *Sesh Uttar* [1942]. But Barua of *Mukti* was quite different from the one of *Sesh Uttar*.[41] The Barua I encountered in *Mukti* was a very strict disciplinarian; his sense of punctuality was rigid too. The time schedule of one's entry–exit and other movements were monitored as in a school.[42] In *Sesh Uttar* the strict disciplinary obligations had slackened. The interest to work had also lessened. A complaint that I harboured deep in mind during *Mukti*, turned into a firm belief now. Director Barua was a superior person than the artist Barua. Barua as an actor had never been able to surpass his abilities as director. Are my words becoming too much of a riddle? I will try to explain.

As a director, Mr. Barua has been the initiator of many new things. Present-day film industry operates following his footsteps. He broke away from the traditional manner of speaking theatrically and began the natural way of delivering dialogues. Movements of the characters became naturalized in the light of reality. It is for this reason that even today when we see his films, his way of speaking, the style he followed does not seem unnatural. Besides there was a modern approach in the way he used the camera and other techniques. He was solely responsible for revolutionizing Bengali cinema.[43] As an artist [actor], however, his thoughts were like any other of his age; nothing was very extraordinary compared to others. For a particular scene if it demanded that the focus of the camera should be on a co-artist so that it could bring out the meaning of the scene better, Mr. Barua was not ready to accept; he preferred to occupy the central part of the frame. If in any scene, he was present, he wanted to dominate the scene entirely through his majestic presence. Such unrestrained behaviour would have suited some other artist, but perhaps not a renowned director like him. As a director, he should have emphasized on the performance of other actors in the film and on greater teamwork. There had always been stiff competition among artists and I must not falter to admit that I was also not outside this. In this case, Mr. Barua being an artist was not spared from such artistic anxiety...

In *Sesh Uttar* several camera angles selected for me for the film were not practically desirable. I had also mentioned this to him. The faults were, however, not rectified.

Yet as a director, I had seen such finesse in his work, which I cannot but respect. ...He had a comprehensive idea about songs and knew how to use them to enhance the drama. ...*Sesh Uttar* had two heroines, Reba [played by

Jamuna Barua] and Mina, the first being modish and progressive, the other simple, pleasant and unpretentious. In a particular scene of the film, in a radio talk or in some speech (I do not remember exactly), Reba says, 'We do not want to remain wild flowers in the darkness of the forest'. Just after that Mina sings, 'I am the flower of the *forest*' ['*Ami banaphool go*']. By using just a single line from the song, the contrast he imparted in the two characters would not be possible to illustrate even with a plethora of dialogues.

During the shooting of *Mukti* I had come in contact with [actor, singer and music composer] Pankaj Mullick. Pankajbabu was a hero in the world of music. I was also an ardent fan of his songs. When I underwent training under him, I became his devoted follower. I noticed with great respect that he not only had a good voice, he had studied *sangeet shastras* [the principles of music] very keenly and had introspected and delved deep into it. Hence his voice had great restrain and softness as well as made a deep emotional impact.

One day, Amar Mullick took me to Pankajbabu's room to take lessons on the songs of *Mukti*. That was the first day I saw him. He was seated on a carpet with his harmonium before him. By his side, arranged in order, were a huge number of books and notebooks of various sizes and colours. He greeted me with a smile. Then he said, 'I will teach you such a song which will remain a precious gift to you for your entire life.'

Pankajbabu had an interesting way of teaching music. He explained the tune and the lyrics in such detail that it struck every chord of my mind. The first song he taught me was, '*Aaj sabar rang e rang meshate habe*'.[44] Before rehearsing the songs, he used to explain Rabindranath's [Tagore's] philosophy and his songs. His words echo in my ears even today. He felt that this song was not meant to be sung for a sequence on *Holi*. It was a devotional piece... He reasoned, 'The screenplay demands to explain that Prashanta is your husband, your happiness lies in his happiness, his fame is your glory. "*Sei rat er swapno bhanga, tomar hriday hok na ranga."* Why should it be painted? This should be your glorification. These colours are not the colours of Holi. It is an expression of love, devotion and respect. ...It is the rasa that is dominant in the song, and which needs to be thought about.'

In this way delineating various kinds of pictures, Pankajbabu would strike a chord in my heart with his melody. With his words in mind, my listeners warmly received whatever I would sing. Besides this, he would always remind me that in *Mukti* the audience will hear Rabindrasangeet [songs of Tagore] in my voice for the first time. So, I need to ensure that the song earns the same respect that these listeners had for the poet's compositions. 'The devotion you express while worshipping God must be evident while singing this song.' As advised, I had maintained caution while singing the song and it was also the reason why it had been accepted so widely. Clear pronunciation, distinctness in every chord of the tune, proper modulation of the voice, expression of the sentiments in each chord were factors about which he was strictly vigilant. The method of teaching followed by Pankajbabu was very orderly and disciplined. He was a real artist. Besides having profound knowledge of the arts, he was very practical. This made him a good artist and an excellent teacher. It is because of this mastery of his that the appeal of his songs holds sway over many generations. His devotion to teaching was profound and his way of appreciating and awarding his students was generous. I came to know that he had awarded me with the title of 'The First Singing Star of New Theatres'. It was a huge reward for me to receive such an accolade from a skilled master like him. In this context it is important for me to mention something.[45]

I could easily pick up the tunes taught by Raibabu or Pankajbabu not because of any outstanding capability on my part but for my tutelage under Ustad Alla Rakha Khan. Two to three years of regular riyaaz had resulted in developing this acumen of mine. It was my basic foundation. The song

'*Aaj sabar rang e rang meshate habe*' had become widely popular across the country as soon as *Mukti* was released. However, my favourite song was '*Tar biday belar malakhani*'. That song would always haunt me. Due to Pankajbabu's guidance, the film connoisseurs also received this number very well. I realized that if one is trained in classical music, rendition of any kind of melodious song becomes easier...Ustad's last words to me would resonate in my ears: 'My girl, you will later realize what you have lost.' ...After *Mukti*, Mr. Barua's assistant Phani Majumdar invited me to act as heroine in his film *Sathi*, opposite K. L. Saigal.

'SATHI AND OTHER FILMS'

The first part of *Sathi* depicted a flooded village, destroyed and devastated, and a young boy and girl, seeking refuge. The movie followed their growing up together, their adolescent years full of fights and friendship, gradually maturing into a romantic bonding in their youth with the little misunderstandings that emerged in their pre-adult minds. This was the main plot that resulted in a happy meeting of the two lovers, surpassing the misunderstandings and conflicts. Bhulua, K.L. Saigal, played the protagonist and I played Manju, his beloved. The novelty of the plot and the songs appealed to me. For the role of Manju, Phani Majumdar had explained the part to me quite well and had left the rest for me to execute. I realized the joy of freedom when shooting for *Sathi*. I had used the experience of these long years to my heart's content. From the film critics to the commoner, everyone appreciated my lively performance in the film. I am indebted to Phanibabu for its success. His greatness as a director lay in his ability to restrain the power to dominate others. From my experience in this film, I realized that this benevolence helps in the total burgeoning of the artist's talent. ...The music director of this film was again Raichand Boral. Raibabu made a new experiment. First, the duet '*Babul mora*' sung by

Saigal and me made it evident to the films enthusiasts that through skillful rendition classical music could also be made popular.[46] Besides in few of the songs, western orchestration was deployed.[47] But [while western instruments were used] for the musical structures and the tunes, the [original and folk] Bengali form was retained. [Thus] Few realized that there was [a western] orchestration for this song. The range of melody moved the audiences. During the composition of the tunes, those of us who were present in the room understood the intricacies from Phanibabu's elucidation.

There was a song *'Tomake harate pari na'* [I cannot lose you]. When one listens to the tune of this song closely, its pace, tones, the manner in which its pitch was made to end on a high note, the variations brought in its melody to reflect and enliven the conflicts—all such details become evident. One would be startled to listen to the songs sung by Saigal.[48] Even today, I remember whenever there used to be a 'take' of Saigal's songs, I would rush from my 'makeup' room leaving aside every other thing. Saigal did not have a traditionally sweet voice. But his all-pervading voice, emotionally charged *mir*, his unparalleled style of rendition attracted me immensely. He also had a magnetic personality. In hours of leisure, he would go on humming tunes and notes standing at one place. Saigal was like a bunch of fresh grass in the heavily cemented huge walls. He was an extremely modest and a superior human being, rare to find.

The quality in Saigal that was sure to move anyone was his humility. From the gatekeeper of the studio to the gardener, whenever he met them, he would ask with a smile, 'How are you? I hope you are keeping well.' He was such a popular artist, so famous, yet never conscious of his stature. With dishevelled hair, betel leaf in his mouth, clad in dhoti and kurta, he seemed like a very ordinary man. I was startled when Mr. P. N. Roy introduced me to him. Is this K. L. Saigal whose songs have always enthralled me? My astonishment vanished when this man with his unusual manners bowed and with folded hands said namaskar. He praised my acting and singing skills as if I were a famous artist. I was so embarrassed that I could not even protest.

I have noticed, while working with Saigal, how he would so easily with a smile on his face, keep himself in the background and bring all other characters to the foreground. Did he ever boast of his qualities? With other artistes, I always felt confident that I could make a better vocal rendition than my co-star though the latter could be a more capable actor. But I could not be so sure when working with Saigal. He was popular throughout India for his songs. Even among the ustads, Saigal, the ghazal singer, was revered. Initially, I was quite nervous when working with him in *Sathi*. But he swept away all my inhibitions, commenting, 'Forget those problems, you sing first.'[49]

As soon as I started singing he remarked in appreciation, '*Wah, wah, kya baat!*' shaking his head, which ushered in a flood of inspiration and enabled me to overcome my fears as well as my anxieties. I suddenly realized that I was not only enjoying singing, but also felt an urge to perform better. I am grateful to Mr. Saigal for encouraging me to give in my best at a time when I felt throttled and insecure, acting within various constraints. I am grateful to this man for inspiring me at that time. Can I ever pay back my debts to him?

During those times, only one microphone was used either for chorus or duet. Whoever sang would try to occupy the position before the microphone. This was normal. But during the 'take' of mine and Saigal's duet song, he would move swiftly and push me towards the microphone. When I would feel embarrassed, he would pat my shoulders and say, 'Not a problem, please go on.' The same would happen in front of the camera. While taking a shot, he would stand in such a manner so as not to attract too much attention. Whenever I would proceed to say something about this, he would point his fingers towards me and say, 'People must see what is to be seen.' Then the studio floor would resonate with his loud laughter. I have never seen such a selfless person.

Saigal was as careless as a truant child. When he made mistakes, none could be angry on him. At times he would be missing from the sets, while a certain 'take' had to be shot. When after a long and patient wait, the unit would be thinking of a pack-up owing to his unavailability, someone would discover him sitting in the last room and singing songs, playing the harmonium, or completely oblivious of the world. When the unit members tried to bring him back to the sets, he would reply, 'Oh! I'm just coming in a while.' Then he would rush back with half of his make-up and arrive on the sets saying, 'Why are you getting angry brother, see I have almost done it.' Saying this he would put a betel leaf in his mouth and sing a ghazal, *'Mere dilme dilke pyara.'* (In my heart, my heart's favourite resides). Instantly thereafter, he would rush back, complete his make-up and enter the sets while tying the pagri. People in the set would roll with laughter. How could they be upset with him?

While working in *Sathi* I had several remarkable experiences. I have mentioned earlier that the film starts with two young children, a boy and a girl, being washed away by the floodwaters. The scene was actually being shot in the waters. Suddenly there was high tide and the surging waters of the tide had washed away the entire unit to various places. For a long time we could not find members from the team. Later someone from the team, who was a good swimmer, rescued them. Though it entailed a lot of risk, often the shoot was an amusing experience. For instance, in that film, a propeller was used to create the impact of a storm on the sets. It so happened that Saigal's wig was blown away by the forceful winds when the propeller was started, thus triggering off much mirth and glee amongst the members of the set. Working for *Sathi* was a spontaneous and beautiful experience for me as it had a vibrant and delightful ambience.

After its release, *Sathi* became very popular. The audience appreciated my pairing with Mr. Saigal in *Sathi*. On 3 December 1938, *Sathi* was premiered at Chitra and New Cinema. *Sathi's* Hindi adaptation, *Street Singer*, was also well received.

The happiness and satisfaction with which I had worked in *Sathi* turned adverse in *Shapure* (the Snake Charmer). The plot of *Shapure* deals with the snake charmers' community and a girl who grows up in that community and dresses up as a man. It is a psychologically complex story dealing with unusual feelings. Like the earlier productions, this film was also very successful at the theatres. However, the background conflicts of the story were terrible which I have not been able to forget even today.

Since childhood I loathed snakes and was frightened by them. I could not tolerate even the sight of dead snakes. I was reluctant to accept the role from the very beginning and requested it to be offered to another actor. But Debakibabu preferred me for the role. It was difficult for me to refuse as I used to receive a monthly remuneration from New Theatres and I did not have the guts to upset the authorities. So I had to get down to the ground with severe disinterest and bitterness. During the entire period of the shoot of *Shapure* and its Hindi version, I was under acute distress.

To do away with my fear of snakes, Debakibabu prepared various kinds of snakes from wood, rubber, paper, and so on, and would hold them before me. Sometimes he would act as if he was throwing them on me. Rubber or paper, even artificial snakes were unacceptable to me as I felt disturbed at the very thought of snakes. Whenever I would see something shaped like a snake, I would run around the entire studio; Debakibabu would follow me, holding on to his model snakes, insisting that I overcome my fears. In the process, I had tripped over several times, hurt my hands, legs and even sprained my ankles, but such occurrences did not desist him from pursuing on his efforts. I can still feel my pain, young and innocent as I was, subjected to such mental torture. Yet at the studio there was no one who protested against this or would suggest relieving me from such sufferings and replace my role with another actor. As heroines we were helpless.

During the Hindi adaptation, a non-Bengali artist played the role initially played by Manoranjan Bhattacharya. He had a huge giant-like frame. During the shots, he would thwack my shoulders while chanting the *mantras*. It was such a painful experience to tolerate all this, for a frail form like me. During the shoot, wherever his rough hands would touch me, it would leave livid marks. I used to wonder would there be any relief to such anguish. When the man would proceed to deliver his dialogue, my face would be covered with his spit. After the 'takes' I would throw up and could eat nothing. But there was no respite. I had to face more such adverse circumstances throughout the shooting of *Shapure*.

I am not describing these events to accuse someone. I narrate these events only to make the readers aware of the difficulties [female] artists faced in our times. I feel happy that in present times the [female] actors are respected. The unhappy times that we had gone through in the early days of the Bengali cinema, especially the difficulties we were made to endure, have not been entirely wasted. I would be happier if the artists, having received such respect, can in their lives, works, thoughts and ways value this honour showed to them by the audience.

There were minimal chances for me, to mingle, make friends and chit-chat with my contemporary artists. Many did not welcome my entry into New Theatres and my achievement as a heroine of many successful films. Perhaps for that reason, people refrained from being friendly with me. They felt it was essential to corner me into an island of solitude and rebuke me with their laughter. To put up with their resistance I had also taken a firm decision of withdrawing myself into a recluse and not opening up. I remember an incident at the Firpos Hotel, Kolkata, where I had met a colleague of mine. I raised my

Kananbala in publicity material of Sesh Uttar

folded hands to a namaskar; she completely ignored me and walked away. The cause for such a response was that she belonged to the high aristocracy; hence, it was much below her status to exchange perfunctory courtesy with a common actor like me. After going through such repeated experiences from all corners, I sought shelter in my own world of imagination and aspirations. I dreaded that any contact with the outer world would make me remorseful, as if, friends, feelings and affection, were not for me.

Malina's spontaneous friendship amidst this hostile atmosphere came to the loving rescue of my encumbered mind.[50] In those days, Malina was a renowned actress. She had acted in comic and in serious characters with equal prowess. I never noticed any arrogance in her. She was unparalleled in her laughter, merry-making and joyous attitude.

Malina and I owned a joint trunk. It contained packets of puffed rice, fried flattened rice, a stove, vegetable knives, bread, butter and various kinds of titbits to eat and cook. In the huge campus of New Theatres, we would sit under the mango tree near the pond and while eating puffed rice with peanuts, speak on various things. We used to exchange the deepest thoughts in our minds.

During those times, two famous actresses were Uma Sashi and Chandrabati.[51] They were the first few names to be regarded as heroines. When I joined New Theatres, Uma Sashi took leave from the film industry. In *Chandidas*, her delineation of Rami had become almost legendary. I can still visualize, Chandra's role as president in the film *Didi*. Dignified roles, which needed a towering personality, suited her quite well. As a whole, it was difficult to find someone as beautiful as her in this profession.

Perhaps due to lack of friends and well wishers, or any other reason, I was an introvert since childhood. The power of the guru could also be a possible reason. When I had leisure, other than listening to music, I would read the *Ramayana* and the *Mahabharata*. I should not hesitate to mention that I also read *Thakurmar Jhuli* [children's fantasy literature]. One of my favourite books was a collection of Japanese folk tales. I would always dream of a picturesque house situated distantly, away from my gloomy life. There would be flowers all around, or at least, it was decorated with beautiful pictures of flowers and furniture. Even insignificant things would appear beautiful and picturesque. The place would not only have the grandeur of the Middle Ages, but also a dreamlike environment.[52]

Since childhood, I have had to come to terms with such stark reality that the very word 'reality' made me shudder. I always wanted to flee away from the real world. I would purchase various foreign magazines and immerse myself in thinking about interior decoration and the art of flower decoration. When I watched English movies, besides noticing their acting, I would also notice the interiors, the staircase, the ways in which the furniture was placed in the room. I would imagine if I owned a house how I would design and decorate it all to perfection—the entrance; the rooms; the kind of flower vases and stands I would place beside the hugely ornamental gateways; how the holders of the wardrobes would be designed, like the [descriptions in] *Ramayana* and the *Mahabharata*, or like rustic bangles, or a silver lotus. Perhaps, one of the walls of the room would be of the colour of rose, then the lanterns would also be of the same colour. The other room would have everything in soothing green. The bedroom however, would have a bluish tinge. Near my head my [Lord] Gopal would be placed. If I place him in the temple, he would move far away from me through various customary practices. ...I would not be able to see the naughty face of my lord whenever I wanted to. My imagination kept me occupied. Was it only the imagination of a home? I also had other kinds of thoughts.

After working in a different company when I joined New Theatres, I was taken aback seeing their way of functioning. In other places, shooting, takes and rehearsals would all be limited to a certain amount of money and time. But at New Theatres shooting took place throughout the day. There would be 'takes' after 'takes'. There would be no limits to rehearsing. In one word, it was a huge and undesirable expenditure. It was a display of New Theatres' uniqueness, a mark of its aristocracy.

The workers of New Theatres may say many things but I would notice with a heavy heart that due to excess, undesired expenditure, the huge establishment was slowly eroding from within. The pomp, show and glamour outside had dazed everyone. Since childhood, I was so well acquainted with sorrow and despondency that I understood that this prestigious institution of Bengal was decaying from within and its resources were getting exhausted. To the utter disbelief of all, the elephant-marked banner gradually progressed towards a great downfall. That day Bengal was destined to face an irreparable loss.[53]

On certain occasions in New Theatres, there would be musical gatherings. There would also be acting [theatrical performances]. I remember, once in a dance drama on *Alibaba*, I and Lila Desai [of *President*, 1936, fame] played the role of Marzina and Abdullah.[54] In such festivals, the *choto laat* [Governor] and other dignitaries would be present.[55] I had sung many times. At times, the programme would also be relayed on the radio. Radio was not so prevalent in those days. Houses, which owned radios, were viewed with respect by others. On special occasions, or for listening to a special

Writing and Archiving the Self: Conversations and Biographies programme, a crowd would gather around such houses. So, the artists whose programmes would be relayed on radio received special prestige.

Once, a charity show was organized to raise funds for the victims affected by floods. On such an occasion, a few words said by Pankajbabu, always remained very dear to me. Panjkajbabu was training everyone to sing for the programme. He told me, 'Choose and decide on a few songs.' I could not decide out of fear and embarrassment. I said, 'What would I sing? I do not know to sing songs specially suited for such occasions.' Pankajbabu stood up and said, 'Bravo [*shabash*] and patted me. Then with bright eyes, he looked at me and said, 'In those few words, your true artistic mind has been revealed.' I looked at him amazed... Similarly, others were also taken aback. He said, 'Did you not understand?' He looked at the others and went on, 'Did you notice that this popular singer from the silver screen could have easily sung a popular number from the movies and won applause. But she never took that route. She was worried that she did not know songs suitable for such occasions. This attitude brings forth the inner spirit of the artist in her. That is why our Kanan has grown up to become a true artist. Her endeavours are successful.' On that occasion, I had failed to hold back my tears after hearing such praises from a man of his calibre. For the first time, I could not hold back my tears in the presence of others.

Now I can understand why I had become so sentimental on the day. Since childhood, misfortunes and adverse situations had made my mind sensitive and fearful of things. I used to fear befriending others, talking to them or even expressing any opinion of mine. Very early in my career I had earned my share of fame and popularity, which were beyond my expectations. Well, for the same reasons I had also received my share of ill repute.

Others used to consider this silent suffering of my inner core as a demonstration of my pride. They went on searching for my faults and inflicting pain on me, thereby deriving a crude satisfaction by being adversely judgmental on me. My inner self, habituated to the usual muck throwing, had been overwhelmed by such a huge and unexpected complement from Pankajbabu.

The period from 1936 to 1940 was the uninterrupted splendid years of my career. *Jawani ki Raat* [*sic. Jawani ki Reet*, Hem Chunder, 1939] in Hindi, after *Shapure*, had consolidated my fame as an actor throughout India. Nazam, whose extremely handsome looks had also been one of the primary reasons of the popularity of the film, was cast opposite me.

Parajay was the Bengali version of the same. Although named *Parajay* (Defeat), the movie had been one of my primary successes. The most important reason for this was the fact that the character I played was very close to my heart. On the one hand, it was a comic portrayal of man's complete devotion towards the illusionary appeals of a young beauty; on the other, it depicted the excitement of the heroine who saw the reflection of her own beauty and attraction in men's lustful demeanour. The travails of a woman humming with a sense of romance and victory at each prospect of a new lover and fashioning a new self at the earliest opportunity is the major theme of *Parajay*.[56] Directed by Hem Chunder, the Hindi version of *Parajay* was released in New Delhi on 8 December 1939. In Kolkata, both the Bengali and the Hindi versions hit the theatres in March.

Kananbala as Vishnupriya in Srigouranga

The character of Anita would not have attracted me much if the scope of her role only had been restricted to playing the illusive and coy mistress playing around with men. When all the out-worldly excitements and waves die down, the deepest resonance of romance glows in a woman's heart who is now left in her state of sorrow; I had felt similar pangs while playing the role of Anita. It was as if without the curious mixture of the comic and the remorse, the audience would not get to view the array of feelings. The regular stack of letters and numerous phone calls from my fans were a proof that my audiences were moved by my portrayal. I accepted each and every praise that I had received from my admirers as blessings of the Almighty. However, the most memorable among them was the wonderful felicitation from a European student from Oxford who had come for a cultural tour. I remember, one day, P. N. Roy introduced me to this young foreigner near *golghar* in the premises of New Theatres. Tall, intelligent, with dreamy blue eyes and golden curly hair, he smiled sweetly with folded hands and said, 'I have never experienced before such an enthralling voice and alluring beauty.' He handed me a colourful card that had a poet's inscription on it. I do not remember the name of this foreign friend since the card is lost. But I have not forgotten the message on the card: 'Charm is a sort of bloom on a woman. If you have it you do not need to have anything else—and if you do not have it, it does not matter what else you have.'

Even earlier, I had been sufficiently complemented for my acting, looks or singing skills, but I was a bit unsure to believe them because of the somewhat gross and formal expressions, which failed to touch my heart. But the complement from this man who had come from a foreign land had all the signature of a genteel connoisseur of the arts. He had a respect for me in his fascinated looks. Probably for these reasons, the incident had left a mark in my mind.

Parajay's songs became popular, especially '*Pran chay chokkhu na chay*'. Though *Parajay* declared me as a clear winner, *Abhinetri* (Actress) directed by Amar Mullick flagged a big failure in my career. *Abhinetri* dealt with a destitute and unfortunate woman finding solace in her lover's shelter. There were no options left for the singer heroine, who had been stripped off her gift of voice because of illness, but to return to her hero in search of a new lease of life. For a self-righteous woman like her to reconcile and to take a step backward could better be considered a fall rather than a defeat. I never wished to act in this role. But the problem was the same. I was on the monthly pay roll of the New Theatres. Therefore, my individual opinion was of little value. The faults in my portrayal became visible in a work that I was doing against my wishes, the result was my dim performance in *Abhinetri*, as compared to my prior hit films. Pahari Sanyal was cast as the hero. Although it was a flop and was my last movie with him after *Vidyapati*, the songs were well received, especially the track, '*Priyo, tomar tulana nai*' [My love, you are incomparable] which was exquisite both in lyrics and tune, and captured my imagination. A particular line in the song, which ran like this, '*Tumi aseem akash ami chiro nadi*' [You are the illimitable sky and I the perennial river], had its strange resonances in my mind. A true man is as boundless and wide hearted as the sky, where the sky finds its reflection in the clear bosom of the river. I used to be immensely touched by such wonderful thoughts.

Advertisement of Bishabriksha *in* Chitrapanji

The movie was released in Kolkata on 20 November 1940. I

have already narrated earlier how *Abhinetri* failed to produce any new chapter in my career and was a cause of anguish. *Harjeet* was its Hindi version.

This was compensated in *Parichay*, my last movie with New Theatres. It had a classical tragic theme of a woman and her relationships with two men in her life. On one hand, she had great respect for her husband, on the other, there was the promising love of the paramour. *Parichay* was the story of the emotional torment undergone by a woman caught between two men. It portrayed the infinite vacuous darkness of solitude among the plenitude. I was able to handle the complexities of the character easily owing to my past experiences with regards to acting as well as in life. All my life I had felt an attraction towards characters with a complex world of inner conflicts. Thus, when playing such roles, I never felt that I was acting. On the contrary, it had always come to me as if my latent agonies were finding an outlet.

The more complex a character I would get, my interest in performing the role would become greater. In this film, Saigal was cast opposite me. Our duet in *Parichay* became a special attraction. Two of Rabindranath's songs, '*Amar hriday tomar apan hather doley*' and '*Amar bela je jay sanjhbelatey*' became much popular and I was the first to record these. Simultaneously, *Parichay* had its Hindi version in *Lagan*. The film was canned in 1940 but was not released before April 1941.[57] *Parichay* was directed by Nitin Bose with Raichand Boral as the music director. This was my first movie under the direction of Nitin Bose. Nitinbabu used to give us a free hand in our acting and bodily movements. His entire attention was towards cinematography. He took special care in composing the angles of the frames and postures of the characters and took careful note on how the situations of the actors would come alive through his compositions. He was of the opinion that an expression of a human being is captured best at unguarded moments rather than when neatly composed because in such moments there is no scope of choreographing one's mood and expression. He was a believer in the principle that art is never an exhibition but a revelation.

In 1941 I won the BFJA [Bengal Film Journalists Association] award for best actress for my role in *Parichay*.

Translated by Madhurima Mukhopadhyay

NOTES

1 Eric Barnouw and S. Krishnaswamy, *Indian Film* (New Delhi: Oxford University Press, 1980): 80.
2 T. M. Ramachandran (ed.), *Seventy Years of Indian Cinema, 1913–1983* (Bombay: Cinema India International).
3 Also see Madhuja Mukherjee. 'Remembering *Devdas*: Travels, Transformations and the Persistence of Images, Bollywood-Style', *Topia, Canadian Journal of Cultural Studies* 26 (Fall 2011): 69–84.
4 *Film India* (June 1940: 52).
5 See Madhuja Mukherjee, 'Travels with *Devdas:* Notes on Image-Essay' (Chayashabda), on *Kaurab Online: Bangla Kabita Webzine* 32 (November 2010); http://www.kaurab.com/kau32/chhaayaashabda.html; last accessed on 27 July 2014.
6 The conversations presented here are Madhuja Mukherjee's personal interaction with Jamuna Barua during 2000–2001.
7 When P. C. Barua made *Devdas* he was already famous for his cinematic ventures (including the introduction of artificial lights during the making of his film *Aparadhi* 1931). He was a member of the Assam Legislative Assembly as well. Barua was literally the handsome prince and heir to a huge estate in Gauripur (Assam). And, as Rani Burra (ed.), *Looking Back, 1896–1960* (New Delhi: The Directorate of Film Festivals, 1981) puts it, 'he shot over 25 films and 50 tigers'. Barua came to Calcutta to study at Presidency College, after which he went for an European sojourn, and was gradually drawn towards filmmaking. He got some informal yet useful training in London, and returned

to Calcutta with filmmaking equipment. In 1931, he set up his own production studio, namely, Barua Pictures Limited. Barua's studio did not survive the competition from big studios and the shifting production conditions. Eventually, three years later, Barua joined New Theatres.

8   Sarat Chandra Chattopadhyay was singularly the most popular and a true representative of early twentieth-century genre of novelists. He wrote mostly novellas, dealing with popular subjects like problems of individuals and society, tradition and modernity, social norms and desires, and so on. Family was one of the key concerns of his novels, where larger issues were displaced on to a 'personal' terrain. He created archetypal bhadralok prototypes and spaces around the city and village. His narrative pattern explored typical novelistic twists and turns as characters travelled long distances (up to Burma), over several years, encountering different people, situations, and so on. Moreover, 'dialogue'/speech style was truly exceptional with multiple connotations, and this influenced popular cinema to a great extent. His narrating style arguably belongs to the 'Dickens school' as he described situations in realistic details. Journeys, self-destructive ('sadist' and 'misogynist') hero, as well, the self-sacrificing ('masochist') heroine are recurring elements of Sarat Chandra novels. Also see Sumit Sarkar, *Writing Social History* (Delhi: Oxford University Press, 1997), for the '*basha*' (nest) and '*bari*' (home) differentiation and accounts on migration.

9   See Madhuja Mukherjee, *New Theatres Ltd., The Emblem of Art, The Picture of Success* (Pune: National Film Archive of India, 2009).

10 Nitin Bose was a famous cinematographer and director of several popular Bengali and Hindi films including *Chandidas* (Hindi, 1934), *Dushman* (Hindi, 1938) and *Ganga Jamuna* (Hindi, 1961). He was well known for his technical innovativeness (along with his brother Mukul Bose they instituted the playback system during the making of *Bhagyachakra*, 1935). Bose emerged as a very popular director after moving to Bombay in the fifties. He was related to the famous scientist Satyen Bose (of the 'Boson' fame) and filmmaker Satyajit Ray. See B. Jha, *Nitin Bose, Flowering of a Humanist Filmmaker* (Calcutta: Asian Film Foundation, 1986).

11 Bimal Roy was a renowned filmmaker and cameraperson who shot to fame after he shifted to Bombay and made landmark films like *Do Bigha Zamin* (1953), *Devdas* (1955), *Madhumati* (1958), *Sujata* (1959), *Bandini* (1963). See Firoze Rangoonwalla, *Bimal Roy, A Monograph* (Pune: National Film Archive, 2009).

12 Pankaj Mullick was an eminent singer, composer and actor. He emerged as an eminent music director with *Mukti* (1937), where he composed the music for a poem written by Tagore. He was trained in Rabindra Sangeet and one of his most memorable films as an actor was *Daktar* (1940), adapted from Sailajananda Mukhopadhyay's *Teen Purush*. With *Mukti* especially, Barua seemingly gave Mullick an opportunity to grow out of his apprenticeship and develop as a creative composer.

13 While, women's reform movements were part of the nineteenth-century socio-cultural changes, the value system of the new patriarchy re-invented the idea of womanhood in opposition to the older patriarchal customs as well as to the westernized woman. The 'women's question' was one of the fundamental subjects of the nationalist discourses. Yet, women's issues were fraught with complexities and anxieties at a moment when women were also receiving western education and learning to assert themselves in disparate ways. Since the (imagined) woman—the basis of the home and culture—had to be 'protected', women's problems became an important aspect within the structure of 'cultural homogenization' of the bhadralok. These were inevitably played out by imposing new kind of norms on the women, whose identity was to be worked in opposition to women from 'uncultured' lower classes (*chotolok*) as well as the westernized woman (*memsahib*). Formal education was thought to be a requirement for the bhadromahila and became acceptable only when it demonstrated that it was possible for a woman to acquire the cultural refinements offered by modern education without jeopardizing her place at home, that is, without becoming a memsahib. The dichotomy of these figures comes up in Barua's *Adhikar* and *Mukti*, even when he was a propagator of liberal values.

14 Also see Kananbala's writing translated here and represented in this chapter.

15 Actually, Barua introduced artificial light during the making of *Aparadhi* (1931), and he had travelled to England before that.

16　Also see Kananbala's biography, *Sabare Ami Nomi*.

17　See *Manoos* (1939) by V. Shantaram, which does a thorough caricature of New Theatres' elaborate musical arrangements.

18　The film *Kaagaz ke Phool* (Dir. Guru Dutt, 1959) fictionalizes the making of *Devdas*, including the limited use of make-up.

19　See Kananbala's writing translated in this chapter. Also see B. Jha, *B. N. Sircar, A Monograph* (Calcutta: NFAI, Pune, in association with Seagull Books, 1990).

20　Uma Sashi joined the film industry during the silent era; earlier she was in theatre. While she joined the stage at a very young age, she became extremely popular with the release of *Chandidas* (Dir. Debaki Bose, 1932), *Ruplekha* (Dir. P. C. Barua, 1934), and so on. Her film *Desher Mati* (Dir. Nitin Bose, 1938) is considered to be one of the earliest social-realist films.

21　See Oral Evidence of Ruby Myers née Sulochana (in *Indian Cinematograph Committee Report*, 1927–28) cited in this volume.

22　Never had so much money been invested so zealously in the Indian film industry, as was the case during the Second World War. Therefore, despite the rationing of raw stock and huge increases in the costs due to higher studio rents and growing fees of the stars, the number of films produced every year went up with the War. Popular films, which ran for four to six weeks earlier, began to run for four to six months. Indeed, the industry experienced an unprecedented and incredible growth. While the cost of production went up six times, the price at which films were sold, even before they were made, increased several times more. New and eager financiers began to join the industry, turning filmmaking into a 'racket'. Raw stocks became limited and with time nothing was accessible except in the 'black market' and at inflated prices. Eventually, the licensing system for films was withdrawn with the end of the War. Meanwhile, small houses became entirely bankrupt and major companies underwent grave financial crisis. Star-actors, star-directors and star-music directors were easily 'bought' with the free-flowing black money. 'Glorious Gohar', who had 15 years of fame and almost half-a-century of hits in the film industry, as the partner of Ranjit Film Studio, said in an interview in 1979 (in Rani Burra (ed.), *Looking Back*: 61): '[i]t's only when freelancing started that the Film Industry became like a Share Bazaar. The highest bid is all that counts now'.

23   By the thirties, big companies came forward with well-equipped studio floors and a set of new (sound) equipment along with skilled technicians. They employed writers, directors and actors (who could sing) on a payroll. An extraordinary business sense, a more organized production-distribution-exhibition system with technical and capital investments (which were several folds higher than the 1920s) was introduced to the film industry. Often many studios hired foreign technicians to train their own personnel as well as to produce 'high' quality films. From the inception of what may be referred to as the 'industry', big studios grew mostly in the metropolitan cities like Calcutta, Bombay, Pune and (sooner or later) in Madras. Thus, along with New Theatres, few self-taught technicians teamed up in Pune, Maharashtra, to set up the Prabhat Film Company. Progressive writers like K. A. Abbas regarded one of its pioneering directors V. Shantaram as the most talented filmmaker of the period. In 1929, along with other technicians Damle, Dhaiber, Fathelal, Kulkarni, he began work in a 'canvas'/tent studio in Kolhapur. Shantaram's *Ayodhyeche Raja* (1932), created a space for Prabhat in film history. In 1936, he made *Amar Jyoti*, but it was with *Sant Tukaram*, in 1937 (which received a Merit award in Venice Film Festival), by Damle and Fathelal that Prabhat created history. *Sant Tukaram* ran in a Bombay theatre for more than a year. Abbas comparing it with *Acchut Kanya* wrote, 'Tukaram flying away on the wings of a bird looked more natural than the obvious town-bred hero driving a bullock cart in a certain very popular film!' (*Film India*, May 1939: 46) Shantaram went on to make socials like *Duniya na Mane* in 1938 and *Aadmi* in 1939. Expressionist films evidently influenced him; his critical approach to tradition and modernist intentions put him as one of the most important directors of the period.

Bombay Talkies was established by two England returned Bengalis trained in visual arts. Himashu Rai and Devika Rani had an unprecedented knack for entrepreneurship. They launched international productions and international releases (including *Light of Asia*, 1924) and benefited considerably from the success of Indo-German productions until the Nazis rose to power and the political situation in Europe changed for the worse. They attempted Anglo-Indian productions as well, however, eventually settled for Bombay, and established their company that became an important training ground for many future stars. One of the most popular Bombay Talkies' films *Acchut Kanya* (1936) was based on populist Gandhian ideals of abolition of untouchability. Bombay Talkies films defined the codes for mainstream Indian cinema like the narrative patterns, the use of song to narrate the plot, use of type characters, pre-given endings and the demands of the stars. Despite these major studios in the big cities, several regional studios came up, presenting their regional identity and pride. For instance, in 1937, Bangalore had 2 studios, Kolhapur 6, Pune 4, Lahore 4, Salem 6, Calcutta 19, Lucknow 1, Tanjore 1, Madras 36, Madurai 7, Nellore 1, Bombay 34, and so on.

24 Eminent singer M.S. Subhalakshmi also did a few male roles in the early talkies, which exploited her singing prowess at a time when talking films became extremely popular and there was a dearth of singing actors.

25 From the autobiography of Kanan Devi, co-authored by Sandhya Sen, *Sabare Ami Nomi* (Kolkata: M.C. Sarkar, 31–68).

26 Radha Films was formally set up in 1932, near Tollygunge, by Haripada Bandyopadhyay and Seth Radhakrishna Chamariya. The Chalachitra Satabarsha Bhavan (Nandan), Government of West Bengal, is now located in its premises.

27 B. N. Sircar's father, N. N. Sircar, was Advocate General of Bengal and later Law Member in the Viceroy's Council. His great grandfather Pyari Charan Sircar was the author of *First Book*, a primary book on English grammar that was studied regularly even in the recent past. Sircar himself was a civil engineer trained in Glasgow, and was trying hard to create a niche in the construction field when he ventured into filmmaking. Sircar's class positioning was a decisive factor in the way New Theatres emerged as one of the most powerful emblem of culture and fitted into the schema of film and nationalist imaginings. Almost immediately with its inception, New Theatres became an important house largely because of its massive investments, up-to-date production systems, studios,

theatres and its personnel. It was regarded to be a cultural institution, a training centre for amateurs and a working space for stalwarts who moved towards New Theatres almost immediately after its commencement. New Theatres created both space as well as a 'literary' aesthetics with which the bhadraloks could identify.

28 *Street Singer* (Phani Majumdar, 1938) seemingly narrates her own struggles. It is the story of Bhulua (Saigal), who wishes to be a performer and is a musician par excellence, and Manju (Kananbala), who is a dancer and a singer. After their arrival in the city while Bhulua's talent is recognized and appreciated, the beautiful Manju becomes a popular singer and actress. The question of market and popular forms, city and urbanization are addressed to the plot. The remarkable song '*Babul mora*', sung in two musical variations by Kananbala and Saigal, respectively, become the 'climax' of the film where these issues merge. See Guru Dutt's comment on *Street Singer* in *Kaagaz ke Phool*. Also see, Neepa Majumdar *Wanted Cultured Ladies Only! Female Stardom and Cinema in India, 1930s–1950s* (New Delhi: Oxford University Press, 2010).

29 Madhuja Mukherjee, 'Early Melodramatic Forms and the Subject of *Bhakti*: Gender, Sexuality, and Modes of Subversion', in *Religion and Popular Culture in the Indian Subcontinent*, Gopa Gupta, Seema Kundu and Shuchismita Mitra (eds.) (Kolkata: Bethune College, 2012: 35–64).

30 Debaki Bose's first talkie *Chandidas* (1932) on the life and poems of the sixteenth-century *Vaishnavite* poet allowed Bose to explore themes that were until then unaddressed in cinema. The film was 'saturated with music' (Barnouw and Krishnaswamy, *Indian Film*: 76). Bose was credited for introducing background music to Indian cinema. Its popularity allowed Bose to make a film on the Punjabi saint *Puran Bhagat* (1933), which put New Theatres on the national map and it gained immense popularity in the North-West frontier provinces. Later, in 1934, Bose's *Seeta* became the first film to be sent to the Venice Film Festival. Bose's fame reached its high point with *Vidyapati* (1937), which revolutionized the concept of film music as it established musical codes for Indian films. While describing his cinema, Debaki Bose stated, 'I am talking about films that

are deeply connected to literature and have become beautiful because these are linked to fine arts like music, dance, acting, etc.' See Ardhendu Sekhar Sengupta, *Debaki Kumar Bose: A Monograph* (Pune: National Film Archive, 2009).

31 Raichand or R. C. Boral was probably the most influential music composer of Indian cinema. Before he joined the New Theatres Ltd., Boral was with the Indian Broadcasting Company. He was trained in North Indian style of music and worked with classical patterns as well as disparate Bengali folk music and *kirtans* (prayer songs) with great panache. He introduced the lyrical ghazal (North Indian) style of singing to the Bengali music scene. Moreover, his treatment of string instruments along with the *shehnai* (Indian 'oboe') and the bamboo flute created the unique music of *Chandidas* (Bengali, Debaki Bose, 1932). Also see Madhuja Mukherjee, 'The Architecture of Songs and Music: Soundmarks of Bollywood, a Popular Form and its Emergent Texts', *Screen Sound Journal* 3 (November 2012): 9–34.

32 Durgadas Bandyopadhyay was a trained artist, who began his career with Madan Theatres. He was popular both as stage and film actor. After he joined New Theatres, he performed in their major productions including *Chandidas* (Dir. Debaki Bose, 1932), *Vidyapati* (Dir. Debaki Bose), and so on. He also worked with other production houses, namely, Sree Bharat Lakshmi Pictures.

33 See Muzaffar Ahmed, *Kaji Nazrul Islam: Smriti Katha*, First edition (Calcutta: NBA Pvt. Ltd, 1965).

34 In the film, the queen, Lakshmi, is mesmerized by *Vidyapati*'s poems as well as his charming persona. However, she knows that this attraction is against the law of the society; moreover, in reality, she respects her husband and is duty bound towards the state and her marriage. Hence, the film becomes the journey of the tormented souls. In *Vidyapati*, everyday situations are not only infused with Vaishnavite poetic traditions but often Vidyapati's poems become dialogues, while his lyrics become a narrative force in the film. Even so, the first lengthy and delicately worked out sequence is one of the most cinematic sequences both in terms of images and music. *Vidyapati*'s long-time companion, Anuradha, takes on the voice of the narrator and comments on the situations. Played by Kananbala,

Anuradha not only declares her love rather unabashedly, her bodily gestures, the ways in which she addresses the camera and articulates her feelings make the film a significant text that speaks about female sexuality and captures her erotic drives.

35 Vidyapati was a medieval Vaishnavite poet.

36 Both Amar Mullick and P. N. Roy were long-time associates of Sircar. Mullick acted in a number of New Theatres' films and directed *Bardidi* (1939).

37 For a discussion on how playback system emerged and became popular, see Madhuja Mukherjee, 'Popular Modes of Address and Art of Playback in Hindi Melodramas', *South Asian Journal* 29 (July–September 2010): 91–104.

38 Perhaps referring to Pankaj Mullick.

39 Madan Theatres Ltd., had ventured into film production at the beginning of the twentieth century. J. F. Madan emerged as one of the father figures of Indian and specifically Bengali cinema. The Madans built Calcutta's first theatre and dominated the scene for about 30 years. Around 1925 and 1926, all Bengali films were Madans' productions. By 1927, Madans' distribution chain controlled half of India's theatre halls. Moreover, Madans initiated the practice of adaptation in cinema and procured the rights of the novels of eminent nationalist author Bankim Chandra Chattopadhyay. By 1927 Madans' distribution chain seized half of India's theatre halls and owned about 172 theatres across British India. Furthermore, the Madans were extremely successful in distributing and exhibiting American films. Despite this, with the coming of sound in the 1930s, this colossal production–distribution–exhibition house was already losing much of its ground. Around 1930, Madans tried to streamline themselves. Earlier in the late 1920s, J. J. Madan, son of J. F. Madan, had visited New York and had seen *Jazz Singer* (1927), where he observed the obsession with singing stars. He got an immediate indication of changing production relations. Since 'J. Madan caught the fever' (Barnouw and Krishnaswamy, *Indian Film*: 65), the Madans imported R.C.A. sound machines, constructed sound compatible studios and recorded certain scenes from contemporary popular theatre. In 1932, Madans did fairly good business, though in 1933 they produced only two (Bengali) films. Transitions from the 1920s to the 30s

in terms of technical development as well as economic and political changes are indicated by the rapid disintegration of small-scale enterprises as well as the steady growth of large-scale studios. Moreover, individual entrepreneurs gradually drifted towards the more structured institutionalized projects.

40 Pahari Sanyal began his film career with New Theatres. An expert singer, Sanyal had a long film career, beginning from 1933 up to 1973. He also acted in Satyajit Ray's films.

41 Kananbala's sweet voice was a significant aspect of her soaring popularity and was highlighted through specific sequences in the film *Sesh Uttar* (P. C. Barua, 1942). In this film, Barua plays the absent-minded zamindar, while Jamuna Barua played his sophisticated fiancée. Kananbala plays an innocent village girl (described as '*banaphool*' or wild flower), whose voice is apparently as good as the sound emanating from the gramophone records.

42 Indeed, New Theatres was notorious for its discipline including regulations regarding maintenance of the time schedule; its canteen food was famous as well; and many stories regarding it became popular. See Pinaki Chakraborty, *Chalachitrer Itihashe New Theatres* (Calcutta: Ananda Publishers, 2006).

43 Barua was clearly one of the most perceptive filmmaker of his times. Besides, his sweeping track shots, as well as the production of unique images in both *Devdas* and *Mukti*, the use of sound and music were imaginative and influential. Guru Dutt's *Kaagaz ke Phool* is seemingly about Barua, in which we see the protagonist shooting *Devdas* (within the studio structure).

44 *Mukti*, in reality was the first Bengali film to use Rabindrasangeet both as a mark of culture as well as to comment on the situation.

45 Both Saigal and Kananbala were extremely popular 'singing stars' of New Theatres. Indeed, both enjoyed a pan-Indian popularity, and Saigal particularly had a mythical status during this time.

46 For a discussion on this song, see Madhuja Mukherjee, 'Early Indian Talkies: Voice, Performance and Aura': 39–61, as well as, Neepa Majumdar, *Wanted Cultured Ladies Only!*.

47 See Madhuja Mukherjee, 'The Architecture of Songs and Music: Soundmarks of Bollywood, a Popular Form and its Emergent Texts', *Screen Sound Journal* 3 (November 2012): 9–34; and Biswaroop Sen, 'The Sounds of Modernity, The Evolution

of Bollywood Film Song', *Global Bollywood, Travels in Hindi Song and Dance*, edited by Sangeeta Gopal and Sujata Moorti (Minneapolis: University of Minnesota Press, 2008: 85–104).

48 K. L. Saigal's first song '*Jhulano jhulao*', sung in Asavari Ghandhari, created history. He had introduced the 'recitative' mode in film song and performances. Saigal rarely used any orchestra, especially for '*Babul mora*', which is performed in pure Bhairavi in the outdoors. He was hugely popular and was truly the first 'pan-Indian male star', whose most admired renditions of the ragas were Yaman, Sindura, while his accompaniments were mostly restrained and evocative rather than loud and assertive. A tanpura, a harmonium, and a tabla would often accompany his songs. Even when there was an orchestra, it was used with restraint. For instance, while singing Kafi, Khambaj or Desh, he would perform a line of alaap, and then break into speech or change the tempo (*laye*) and the emphasis (*tal*), and surprise the audience as in *President* or *Devdas*. Associating speech with music became a feature of his star persona, along with his comic sense. There was indeed not much singing in the songs like '*Sukh ke dukh ke ab din bitat nahi*', or in '*Ek bangla bane nyara*' where he included rhymes. While the constant shift from music to speech was a remarkable recording achievement in 1935; his 'nasal' rendition with a tragic grandeur had its own style and appeal. The poignancy of the narrative of *Devdas*, the way he approached despair, sorrow and death is attained through Saigal's singing. When he sang the famous thumri, '*Babul mora*' with the third note on the harmonium as the root key (E-note), it created unique resonances.

49 See R. R. Menon, *K. L. Saigal: The Pilgrim of the Swara* (New Delhi: Hind Pocket Books, 1989).

50 Malina Devi was a trained dancer and followed similar routes as other (female) actors of the times. She first joined Minerva Theatre, followed by a short stint with Star Theatre. Eventually, she joined New Theatres after having worked with Madan Theatres and Radha Films. She was also the co-actor of Ratan Bai (see Chapter 2). She did a comic role in *Sharey Chuattor* (Dir. Nirmal Dey, 1953).

51 Chandrabati Devi was one of the few actors who had formal education and studied in school and college. She had a

towering personality and acted in several New Theatres films, and often played powerful (negative) characters. Gouranga Prasad Ghosh (1982: 113) in *Sonar Daag* (Calcutta: Jogomaya Prakashani) describes her as 'the first female producer'.

52 The idea of an imaginary home or house is a recurring theme in Meena Kumari's poems as well. See translation included in Chapter 3.

53 See memoir of Durga Khote, *I Durga Khote* (New Delhi: Oxford University Press, 1976) republished in 2007; also refer 'Introduction'.

54 The 'Alibaba and Forty Thieves' was a popular plot. While Hiralal Sen adapted it to cinema, Madhu Bose modified the story in 1937. Featuring the society lady, Sadhana Bose (granddaughter of the nineteenth-century reformer Keshab Chandra Sen, who was critical about popular entertainments), the film adapted a well-known *Arabian Nights* story. Undoubtedly, with *Alibaba*, Bengali cinema had its first large-scale spectacle with horses, huge sets, massive orchestration (by T. Fritzpolo) and elaborate dance sequences (choreographed by Sadhana Bose). The plot involved curious intersections between a series of sinful acts (like greed) on the part of the different characters, namely, Ali, Kasem and the leader of the bandits. The slaves, Marjina and Abdullah, had their respective drives as well. Marjina, the young beautiful slave of Kasem, who eventually becomes the dancer in Ali's court and is later married off to his son, is a crucial character in the plot, with a specific function in the resolution. There have been various adaptations of the *Alibaba* narrative in other languages. The booklet of *Daku ka Ladka* of Sree Bharat Lakshmi Pictures advertised the film as, 'Coming shortly/Alibaba/see/Sadhana Bose and All Society Cast/ Direction Modhu Bose'. Moreover, *Dipali* (February 1937), the popular journal of the period, described Sadhana Bose as the 'new star', while the film was substantially praised by the respectable press.

55 New Theatres' publicity journal *Chitra*, October–November 1935, 1.5, published photographs of the programme held on 31 December (?), during which as the original caption states, the 'Viceroy, Countess of Willingdon, Governor of Bengal, the Commander-in-Chief, Maharaja of Burdwan, Prince of

Hyderabad, Duchess of Richmond and other dignitaries' were present.

56 Much of this resonates in Mae West's article re-visited in Chapter 3.

57 The press was critical of these films. For instance, *Film India* (June 1941) wrote the following:

Nitin's *Lagan* is certainly [a] better picture that[n] *Har Jeet* and *Andhi* but is too poor in comparison with his own *Dushman* and nothing to write home about considering the old standard of New Theatres.... .

THE PROBLEM OF RESPECTABLE LADIES: LETTERS AND RESPONSES

2

Ratan Bai had written an 'open letter' to the director and managing director of New Theatres regarding her role (or absence of it) in the film *Karwan-e-Hyat* (also *Karwan-e-Hayat*) (1934). The publicity officer of New Theatres Ltd., belted out a scathing reply, and actor Ratan Bai responded to it through *Picture Play*, February 1934. These letters, originally written in English,[1] were re-published in a Bengali periodical *Chitrapanji*.[2]

The letters raise a few pertinent questions regarding history, materiality of history, historiography and archival projects. While on the one hand, there is little or no information regarding Ratan Bai aka Miss Imambandi, on the other, New Theatres Ltd., as discussed earlier, was a pioneering and bhadralok studio from Bengal which made a specific kind of 'literary' film. It had a particular status in society owing to two essential factors. First, the stature of its proprietor B. N. Sircar, son of the Advocate General of Bengal, as well as its illustrious associates, including directors like P. C. Barua, Debaki Bose (also National Congress activists), cameraperson Nitin Bose, maverick music composers R. C. Boral and Pankaj Mullick, thespian Sisir Bhaduri, Nobel Laureate Rabindranath Tagore, ceaselessly popular author Sarat Chandra Chattopadhyay, exceptional writer Kazi Nazrul Islam and others. Second, its style of filmmaking involved Bengali bhadralok (cultural and economic) investments. For instance, Dilip Sircar, son of B. N. Sircar, during a personal communication (in 2000) commented, 'When a child is born in Bengal, he/she hears three names—Rabindranath, Mohun Bagan [football team] and New Theatres.' Thus, within the context of New Theatres' magnificent stature and the ways in which New Theatres has been repeatedly studied, these letters show the problems of linear history writing and present to us more intricate histories of the times.

Karwan-e-Hyat, the concerned film, is an oriental tale of a vagabond prince who wanders amongst the gypsies. Ratan Bai plays Zarina, a gypsy girl, who is in love with the prince. The prince, performed by Saigal, eventually falls in love with a princess, woes her and in time abandons his gypsy friends. The flirtatious prince and his final 'betrayal' appear allegorical in the present context, and seem like an allegory of the deception of the industry that Ratan Bai suffered. Shot in real palaces, the film has an exceptional rawness that is charming and intriguing. Ratan Bai's soulful songs and performance create unique resonances; moreover, the male actor Nemo, who plays an elderly gypsy woman (described as a witch), makes the film a curious text about gender and desire.

'LETTERS TO NEW THEATRES': RATAN BAI

Dear Sir,

New Theatres-New India picture 'Karwan-e Hyat' was released at the Minerva Talkies on the 26th instant.[3]

As I appeared in the role of the heroine, I was very much anxious to see the picture.

To what extent I was surprised after seeing the above film is beyond description. My four songs and acting in the first portion have been cut off and not only that but another person is appearing in these scenes with the same songs and settings and in the latter half my part has been kept intact.

May I enquire of you, sir, why you have done this? When I was leaving New Theatres all my acting and singing pieces were seen and you informed me that everything was all right and I was given leave to go.

Since my coming away to Bombay you have cut my part in two portions and divided the role in two characters. By doing this are you trying to injure my career.

Will you be good enough to enlighten me on the point?

Yours faithfully
Ratan Bai

The Problem of Respectable Ladies: Letters and Responses

MR. P. ATORTHY WRITES TO US [*CHITRAPANJI*]

I feel my bounden duty to inform the cinema-going public that I am in no way responsible for the merits and demerits of the New Theatres-New India picture which is being shown at present at Minerva Cinema in Bombay, styled as 'Karwan-e-Hyat'. The picture that I directed is not this. Scenes have been changed, a new role has been introduced after my leaving the Company which in my opinion has changed the trend of the story which I conceived.

Although the New Theatres Limited have very kindly put my name with another man, who acted as one of my assistants during the shooting of the same picture, as a director on the credit title, I decline to accept such honour or credit, if there is any ... .[4]

Premankoore Atorthy[5]

New Theatres replied to Ratan Bai's allegations through a journal, *Varieties Weekly*. Ratan Bai retorted back through *Dipali*. *Chitrapanji* republished both letters in consecutive issues.[6]

NEW THEATRES' RESPONSE

Dear Sir,

I am instructed by Mr. B. N. Sircar to request the courtesy of a little space in your esteemed weekly, in order to reply through you to Miss Ratan Bai, apropos her open letter to our Managing Director, published in some up-country [elite] papers.

As a fact our Managing Director usually find it beneath his dignity to take cognizance of a letter, of the type written by Miss Ratan Bai, unless the courtesy of a copy of such a letter being forwarded to him has been extended by the writer. Nevertheless, Mr. Sircar desires on this occasion to make an exception, in view of the fact, that, it strikes him that Miss Ratan Bai is suffering from certain delusions which it would be to her benefit to eradicate at the earliest opportunity.

Miss Ratan Bai hints darkly of such things as revenge, ruination of her career etc. etc. on the part of our Managing Director. I presume, that this attitude on her part is due to the fact that she has not been long enough in the Cinema industry to realize, that, it is not only beneath a Producer's dignity to attack either directly or indirectly one of his ex-actress, but also that, so far as he is concerned, it is a waste of time and cheap past time in any event.

Miss Ratan Bai flatters herself and certainly appears to have an exaggerated opinion of her importance in the film industry, when she hints at a special action being taken against her, in particular by the New Theatres' organisation. She forgets that others holding far more important positions, than she has ever done, have left this concern both before, with and after her, and no particular action has ever been taken either to deride, vilify or belittle them in any manner whatsoever.

So far, it is not our desire to go into the rights or the wrongs of the circumstances under which she left the New Theatre' [sic] banner but she is surely aware of the fact that under the terms of her contract, our Managing director [sic] had the sole right to exercise his option of prolonging her services for another year on the same terms as those under which she had been working. It seem [sic] a little strange that he should have so willingly released her at her very first request for such release! Therefore her assertion that Mr. Sircar was very pleased with her services seems to fall a little flat and bags [sic] a question. Where her complaint of the particular picture 'Karwan-e Hayat' is concerned, she and all those who have worked with her should know very well that every producer reserves to himself the right to make any changes he may consider necessary for the improvement of a picture produced under his banner and such change may involve deletion or addition of certain scenes. So far as our Managing Director is aware and I hope it will be admitted that he more than any other person, should know, the real heroine of the picture 'Karwan-e Hayat' is the Princess of Vijoynagar [Vijaynagar] played by Miss Rajkumari. Therefore, any deletion of scenes played by subsidiary characters is after all of minor importance.[7]

In conclusion, I would remind Miss Ratan Bai that New Theatres and its Managing Director consider with pride the fact so that many of its erstwhile star and directors should have been so eagerly snapped up by other concerns and it seems rather contradictory for Miss Ratan Bai to complain of our Managing Director seeking to ruin her reputation as a star, when it was New Theatres who picked her up as Miss Imambandi of 216, Bow Bazar Street and made of her Miss Ratan Bai of 'All-India' fame. Does it not seem an irony that even now Miss Ratan Bai should be announced as the star of *Yahoodi-ki-Larki* fame? Under our Managing Director's instructions I am forwarding a copy of this letter to Miss Ratan Bai, purely as an act of courtesy, and also to certain papers in Northern India. I trust that unseemly observations on the part of those who have made their name through New Theatres and New Theatres alone will in future be arrested after perusal of this letter. So far as we are concerned, the matter is now closed and we do not desire any further correspondence or controversy over it.

We have also seen Mr. Premankur Attorthy [*sic*] statement (now being advertised as of 'Yohoodi-ki-Larki' [*Yahoodi ki Larki*] fame) and we think it unworthy of any serious attention.[8]

Yours faithfully
For The New Theatre Ltd
Hemanta Kumar Chatterjee
Publicity Officer

RATAN BAI'S REPLY

Dear Sir,

The New Theatre Limited's letter of 9th February was read by me with interest.

It is quite evident that Mr. Sircar is highly displeased with one or two questions regarding my part in 'Karwan-E-Hayat'. The displeasure can be well judged by the very tone of the letter and various remarks made about me in the same, which has no bearing on the subject matter. My letter was couched in a very simple language, the purpose, of which was to ascertain why my part has been cut in two portions and two characters have been made of my one part. This was a simple question which only requires simple answer.

Mr. Sircar's publicity officer writes to say that the Managing Director of the New Theatres Ltd. has the right to do anything he likes with any part. This statement itself serves my purpose as they have therein admitted the fact of omitting my songs and actions. Whether these changes have been made for the so called improvement of the picture or for any other purpose is best known to those who have not only once but so many times seen the pieces. In any case the fact remains that my part has been divided in two characters, and the cine-going public knows that my part has been changed.

Whether Mr. Sircar was satisfied with my services or not is a matter too big and lengthy to be discussed here. Why should I take it otherwise when Mr. Sircar issued a letter to me asking to continue my services for another year? My letter of resignation and its reply will speak for itself.

Whether my part in 'Karwan-E-Hayat' was of a hero-ine or of a side character can be well judged from the story in the booklet published by the New Theatres Ltd., and if this is not sufficient may I draw the attention of the authorities to their advertisements in all Indian papers, before my leaving their concern. Of course, after my leaving the New Theatres Ltd., the matter of their

The Problem of Respectable Ladies: Letters and Responses

advertisement has been changed and the reason for that is not difficult to find.

The concluding paragraph is really very interesting. Mr. Sircar has laid much stress on the point that I have been picked up from Bowbazar Street before which I was a nonentity [sic] and from Imambandi they have made me Ratan Bai of all-India fame. Did I ever approached [sic] the officials of New Theatres Ltd., to give me a job or they approached me to join their company? I hope Mr. Mullick has not forgotten the day he came with the director to my poor abode and his request to join New Theatres Ltd., as they had failed to secure a heroine for 'Subeh-Ka-Sitara' even in Lucknow or other up-country cities.[9]

May I enquire, whether they 'picked up' or not hundreds of persons from Sonagachi, Rambagan, Harkata Gully, Bow-bazar etc., [red-light areas] and how many of them have acquired all-India fame? Was I only made to stand before a camera of the New Theatres Ltd., and down came upon me all-India fame? Do they mean to say that I did nothing in 'Yahoodi-ki-Ladki'? It is so easy to get all-India fame without one having any talent? Can any producer make any successful picture without the artistes doing anything in it? Then again whatever money they have spent on my publicity amounts to a negligible sum in comparison to other producers.

Mr. Sircar seems to be carried away too far in his hatred towards me to indirectly throw hint on me to be of low birth. It is true that I do not belong to that social status as he is, but there is no reason why I can't be an artiste with talent. I may not be in the film line longer than Mr. Sirear [Sircar], but is that an answer to my letter?

It is no use showering indirect abuses on me for the simple reason that I asked why my part has been cut off, and now that the admission has been made I think I have achieved my end and cleared my position.

Yours faithfully
(Sd.) RATAN BAI

Ratan Bai with Saigal and Pahari Sanyal: love and deceit

In *Sonar Daag*, Gouranga Prasad Ghosh narrates in length the life of Nirada Sundari, a 'forgotten' star, from this era.[10] Apparently, Nirada Sundari started her career on stage (with the enigmatic playwright Girish Chandra Ghosh); she was extremely popular and acted in rather successful stage shows as well as in several silent films. However, later she had an accidental fall from the stage, which caused permanent physical disability. In this accident, she almost lost her leg and gradually her eyesight as well. Eventually, she took refuge at a fellow actor's house (Shanti Gupta), and at the age of

The Problem of Respectable Ladies: Letters and Responses

90 she was found penniless and terrified by Ghosh. This particular story becomes further consequential, as we locate somewhat unwittingly her name on the title of *Krishna Kanter Will* (Jyotish Banerjee, 1932) and scan the black and white faces to make meaning of the unaccounted history of Indian cinemas. The film immediately seems to open up a Pandora's box throwing up a plethora of questions regarding cinema, its location in the mesh of historically significant narratives and the manner in which many actors contributed in the making of the films, and yet were lost in oblivion.

As discussed elsewhere, the 'morality machinery' was extremely powerful and persuasive.[11] Thus, one is not surprised when Amar Mullick (the person who apparently requested Ratan Bai to join New Theatres) states in *Varieties Annual* (January 1934: 7), '[w]e cannot expect to produce a heavenly picture like *Songs of Songs* with artistes recruited from the slums of north west Calcutta. It is a happy sign that the pick of society has come into the producing branch of the industry.' Indeed personal lives of most of the actors of this period are fraught with such ambiguities. Some earned respectability through marriage and only a handful gained respect by becoming stupendous stars and producers. As described by Kananbala and Jamuna Barua, the entire milieu in the studios was feudalistic and women actors were rarely considered to be a decision-making agency. Ratan Bai tells us the ways in which hundreds of persons from 'Sonagachi, Rambagan, Harkata Gully, Bowbazar etc.,' or other red-light districts of Calcutta, joined the industry; yet, and, 'how many of them' have survived and have become actors who were respected for their work?

Indian Cinema, Contemporary Perspectives, edited by Samik Bandyopadhyay, addresses an extremely interesting debate on whether 'respectable ladies' should or should not join cinema.[12] For instance, an article written by an anonymous lady artist on the plight of her fellow women actors in the industry evoked a response from Sabita Devi, who explored the subject of respectability, which was one of the primary concerns of the early period.[13] Surely, large sections of popular press insistently dealt with the topic of 'respectability' of the female actors, their background, and present lifestyles, as well as questions of their everyday activities, marriage, chastity, and various other moral issues pertaining to their personal lives. For instance, the June–July 1937, issue ([6]9) of *Chitrapanji*, published a series of articles which bring up subjects like 'Vulgarity in Films', 'The Trap of Cinema', 'Women in Films', 'Actresses', and so on. Similarly, the *Puja* special of the same periodical, in the same year, brought out articles, which were concerned with subjects like 'Film and Sex'. The July–August 1936, issue ([5]10) of *Chitrapanji*, further published an article titled 'Should Women Dance or Not?' as well as articles that mentioned the Censor Board, educational films, and so on. Neepa Majumdar deals in detail with issues of the 'Morality and Machinery of Stardom' also showing how gossip worked in the production of stardom and the ways in which the private lives of the female actors became a recurring topic.[14]

In this volume, the focus is on the stars and their work. Sabita Devi, a poet and an actor, whose article has been anthologized here,[15] was discovered by actor-director Dhiren Ganguly. She had also worked with P. C. Barua.

'WHY SHOULDN'T RESPECTABLE LADIES JOIN THE FILMS': SABITA DEVI

The recent call for a Bengal society film acted by 'respectable society ladies in Bengal' seems to have evoked a storm of disapproval, resulting in the article, I was very pained and surprised to read several weeks back in my copy of [the film magazine] *Filmland*. The contributor, a 'Lady Artiste' veiling her identity, has chosen to attack a whole industry yet in its infancy at a time when it needs our greatest support and co-operation. If this 'Lady Artiste' has had the misfortune to come across only the bad in the screen line, as there is good and bad in every profession, it does not justify her damning the film concerns throughout Bengal, for I, on the contrary, have always been treated with the greatest respect and courtesy during my three years as a screen artiste; and in contributing this article I am doing so not as propaganda, or with any ulterior motive, but for the purpose of defending myself and the good name of many fine gentlemen and friends I have had the pleasure of meeting and working with in the film world.

My first year in 'filmland' in 1929 was spent at the British Dominions Studio at Dum Dum, where I and my mother, who always accompanies me, were shown every respect and consideration and it was only to better my prospects that I left British Dominions Films the following year for the role of Saroj in *Kanthahar* at Indian Kinema Arts with whom I have just renewed my contract, conditions being so satisfactory. Then Indian Kinema Arts kindly lent my services to the Barua-Arya Films for the lead in their *Aparadhi*, and in this studio too, my experiences were only of the best. I have always found my principals and co-workers to be thorough gentlemen, who in trying to embody the aspiration of the West with those of the East, still hold to the traditions of the East in respect of their attitude towards women.[16]

In touching upon this moral aspect of the Studio, may I draw the attention of my readers to the mid-Victorian conception of ladies of the stage which came in for so much criticism during the last century. But as times changed, ideas changed accordingly, and that the same people later appreciated their art and their calling. It is true, on the other hand, due to the dearth of respectable actresses in Bengal, some of the lesser lights [stars] in filmland have been recruited from the lowest strata of society, but for this reason prospective artistes should not be deterred by having to appear in the same picture as these unfortunate women; the sooner they realise that it is far nobler to sympathize than to criticise, this difficulty can be overcome.[17]
During the time of my activities in the various studios, I

have come in contact with these people, yet have found them always quiet and reserved while waiting [for] their turn, or on the 'set'. As artistes, we are not concerned with the private life of an individual whom we have to meet purely in a business capacity, rather are we [sic] concerned with the attitude and behaviour of that person during working hours.

Presuming your contributor to be a lover of her art, I fail to see how she can call herself 'A Lady Artiste' and at the same time try to alienate the minds of others from the films. She talks of 'weak and helpless' girls being at the mercy of unscrupulous libertines, the film actors and producers; she talks of luxury and passion as if they were the be-all and end-all of life, forgetting for the moment that man is not the only actor in this complicated matter of the sexes. The old story of Eve tempting Adam is just as true today as it was a thousand years ago; history repeats itself, and Eve still wields her subtle influence over men more often for evil than for good.

The attitude a man takes towards a woman is governed by the latter's own integrity of character, by her actions, her words and her manner; if she be true, womanly and modest, no man can approach her in any other spirit than that of the deepest reverence and respect, and in my opinion no man is so bereft of these instincts which help in recognising true womanhood, than to dare approach her in any but the manner I have described above. This has always been my happy experience, and I would accordingly urge the society girls of Bengal who are interested in filmland, to see for themselves its fascination and beauty, and that all studios are not as black as they are painted. If a girl has

Sabita Devi, in the magazine *Filmland*

The Problem of Respectable Ladies: Letters and Responses

ability, charm of manner, and screens well, she can go far on her own merit if she has the courage to break through the barriers of convention, take a chaperon with her, and learn for herself that the filmworld is not merely a fairy world of make-believe, but a land that holds promise of great things if she is willing to work honourably and nobly for them.

In closing, I take the opportunity of inviting this 'Lady Artiste' to pay a visit to my studio at any time she may find convenient, when I shall be pleased to show her that the interior workings are not corrupt, that the actors and the principals are gentlemen of the East in the truest sense of the word, and that actresses have not flung 'their morals to the air'.

NOTES

1 The letters have been represented here as they appear in English in the original.
2 *Chitrapanji*, (4)5, February–March 1934: 214–15.
3 This date does not match with the official date as noted in B. Jha, *B. N. Sircar: A Monograph* (Calcutta: NFAI, Pune, in association with Seagull Books, 1990).
4 Co-directed by Hemchandra Chunder.
5 Premankoore Atorthy was the editor of *Nachghar* and wrote popular literature like *Mahastabir Jatak*, and so on. He also made films like *Abataar* (1940) with Sree Bharat Lakshmi Pictures. In such films, time–space was curiously convoluted; he mixed the comic situations with mythical elements and social causes.
6 From *Chitrapanji*, (4)6, March–April 1934, 264–68.
7 Rajkumari played Chandramukhi in Barua's *Devdas* (1935).
8 Atorthy directed *Yahoodi-ki-Larki*.
9 Kananbala also writes in detail about Amar Mullick, actor and long-time associate of New Theatres. He collaborated with B. N. Sircar even before New Theatres was set up. Initially Sircar, Mullick and P. N. Roy started production under the 'International Film Kraft' banner.
10 *Sonar Daag* (Calcutta: Jogomaya Prakashani, 1982: 40, 41).

11 In 'Of Bhadromahila, Blouses, and "Bustofine": Re-viewing Bengali High Culture (1930s–40s) from a Low Angle', *Popular and Visual Culture: Design, Circulation and Consumption*, edited by Clara Sarmento and Ricardo Campos et al (Cambridge: Cambridge Scholars Publishing: 145–66, 2014).

12 *Indian Cinema: Contemporary Perspectives from the Thirties* (Jamshedpur: Celluloid Chapter, 1993); also see Introduction.

13 The problem of respectability comes up persistently and is reflected in the interviews with actors as cited from ICCR 1927–28 (see Chapter 4).

14 Neepa Majumdar, 'The Morality and Machinery of Stardom', Wanted Cultural Ladies Only! Female Stardom and Cinema in India, 1930s–1950s (New Delhi: Oxford University Press, 2010).

15 'Why Shouldn't Respectable Ladies Join the Films', *Filmland* (2)84, 7 November 1931: 4–5; article represented as in the original.

16 While Ratan Bai emphasizes on her skill and stresses on being accepted on the basis of her ability to sing (well), Sabita Devi refers to the problem of respectability.

17 Also see ICCR oral evidences (Chapter 4).

WOMEN WRITING CINEMA: VOICES AND VERSES

3

Poems penned by Meena Kumari, one of the most enigmatic actors of the Indian screen, illustrate her manifold crises at the time she was a reigning star. I take her life, along with her most famous film *Pakeezah* (Dir. Kamal Amrohi, 1972), as reflective symbols, which show the routes female performers, particularly at that time, traversed, in order to obtain their due. Arun Khopkar's writing examines her star persona as well.[1] Moreover, I argue that the collaborations with her (estranged) husband, writer-director Kamal Amrohi, as well as friend and fellow-writer Gulzar produced a series of films and writings, which may be studied as parallel texts. Meena Kumari's poems are testimonies of the range of her abilities, as well comment on star narratives.[2]

Nargis, performed by Meena Kumari, writing in Pakeezah

TANHAA CHAAND
by Meena Kumari (Naz)

Chaand tanhaa hai aasmaan tanhaa.
Dil milaa hai kahaan kahaan tanhaa.
Bujh gaii aas chhup gayaa taaraa.
Tharatharaataa rahaa dhuaan tanhaa.
Zindagii kyaa isii ko kahate hain.
Jism tanhaa hai aur jaan tanhaa.
Hamasafar koii gar mile bhii kahiin.
Dono chalate rahe tanhaa tanhaa.
Jalatii bujhatii sii raushanii ke pare
Simataa simataa saa ek makaan tanhaa.
Raah dekhaa karegaa sadiyon tak.
Chhod jaayenge ye jahaan tanhaa.

THE LONELY MOON

The moon is lonely, so is the sky.
The heart travels the world alone.
Hope is lost, and the stars are hidden.
And, the fire trembles here alone.
Is this what life is?
Where both the body and the soul
are lonely?
Even when I found my companion,
We walked the course separately.
Beyond the lonely quivering light
There is small room standing alone.
I will wait for ages
Before I leave the world alone.

Meena Kumari as represented in a promotional booklet on Pakeezah

TUKRE TUKRE Meena Kumari (Naz)	BIT BY BIT
	The day has passed in bits.
Tukre tukre din bita.	The night came to me in shreds.
Dhajji dhajji raat mili.	[However] we are given
Jiska jitna anchal tha	as much as we can carry.
Utni hi suagad mili.	Every time I tried to know myself
Jab chaha dil ko samjhe	A sound of laughter came from within.
Hasne ki awaaz suni.	As though someone is pronouncing
Jaise koi keheta ho	Hey, you have been defeated again.
Le phir tujhko maat mili.	What is defeat? And, what is beating?
Maatein kaisi, ghaate kya	I keep moving through the shifts of the day.
Chalte rehena, aat peher.	[And] when I found a companion close to
Dilsa saathi jaab paaya	my heart
Bechaini bhi saat mili.	[This] disquiet came along with it.

The most iconic female actor and writer Mae West wrote an open letter through the western [American] weekly *Picturegoer* (Malcolm D. Phillips). Ramendranath Dey translated it in Bengali for *Chitrapanji*, which insisted that reading this article Mae West's Bengali fans would be able to contest her critics.[3]

"আমি-একজন খারাপ মেয়ে"
শ্রীমতী মে ওয়েস্ট - - -

মালকম ডি. ফিলিপস্ বিদেশী সাপ্তাহিক
'পিক্চার গোয়ার' মারফৎ শ্রীমতী মে
ওয়েস্ট-কে একখানি খোলা চিঠি দেন।
বর্তমান প্রবন্ধটি সেই খোলা চিঠির
উত্তরের বঙ্গানুবাদ। প্রবন্ধটি পড়ার
পর মে ওয়েস্ট-এর ভক্তরা আশা করি
শ্রীমতীর শত্রুদের সঙ্গে জোর গলায়
তর্ক করতে পারবেন।

The translation of Mae West's note as published in Bengali for Chitrapanji

'I'M A BAD GIRL'

Many are of the opinion that I'm not a 'good' girl, that I have scaled the peaks of fame through a number of immoral activities. I do not wish people to misunderstand me. The defamation I have gained by acting in films far outweighs the wealth I have earned. But I want everyone to know that I have become immune to such slanders. I like both the wealth as well as the criticisms hurled towards me.

Had such attacks been somewhat balanced, I would not have much to complain about them that are published incessantly in various newspapers. Indeed, it is a fact that I have enacted a particular kind of women on screen, who have sacrificed reputation with a smile. There is no denying of the fact that the good girl cannot offer any satisfaction or joy to the so-called morally upright audience or writers through her acting skills.

I'm not arguing that virtue or honesty is worthless. But it has no place within the materialistic world of cinema. Men like those women who are romantic and are willing to flirt. Women too like such excitements, though none is willing to express this in public.

I know the history through my life. I have read in books about famous women and their colourful lives. While contemporary critics bad-mouthed them, they have been immortalized in history.

I have read the biographies of a number of historically famous women attentively. Hollywood scriptwriters focus exclusively on brilliant love stories revealing the immaculate aspects of personalities like Cleopatra, Salomé, Catherine the Great, Mary, Queen of Scots, Mme du Barry, Mme de Pompadour, Nell Gwyn, and so on. But you and I have read the scurrilous stories that punctuated their eventful lives. If I were to make films out of such stories then a veritable revolt may start all over the world. You are all familiar with their names and the various tales of their degradation. There were innumerable 'good' girls too in those times, but their names have been irretrievably lost in the course of time. Only the 'bad girls' remain immortalized in history. As I was saying, men cannot help loving a girl if they come to know of her disrepute.

Let this not mislead you into thinking that women who live such eventful lives are happier than those who lead dreary, uneventful lives. This is not true; after all, the culmination of the lives of the former group is always lamentable. The only reason I speak of 'bad women' is because people seem to show more interest in the lives of bad girls—people are found to be more eager to listen to the stories of, and associate with, such women.

A lot has changed in recent times. These days, there are so many girls who are pretty but dumb! In my opinion, it is better to be pretty and dumb than be merely dumb. I want to tell the girls: You cannot afford to be dumb today. And, it is possible for a woman to be unpredictable and seductive without being immoral. In business, politics, science and arts, they have rights equal to those of men.

People attack me viciously because I portray sex forthrightly on screen. If I had represented it through a veil of literary conceit and mystification, perhaps, it would have come across as less terrifying. This is something I completely fail to understand because sex is not necessarily vulgar. I don't think it is any more so than eating. Sex is never vulgar except to vulgar people.

I do not comprehend of what use it is to rail against nature. As such, I get worried about my detractors sometimes. My job is to impart some joy to the people by means of my acting skills, and it is 'the people', who have appreciated my work.

I have been often asked to define love. I am incapable of doing so. For, love is such an ethereal thing that it eludes the comprehension of common human beings. But love is a woman's stock in trade and she always ought to be overstocked. Can you hide your heart's desire in a shroud of pretense? Cine-goers who know of their heart's desire cannot but love my films. The characters I play are authentic, flesh-and-blood portraits of real women as we know them. Before the public eye, I trade in matters that are absolutely essential in life, concerns that are not new fangled but are age old.

If you are interested to know about my private life, then I can tell you this—I'm no angel. Who's going to carry the weight of the wings? But I'm happy and you could compare my life with the normal life pattern of any woman. I do not drink or smoke. I do not like the taste of alcohol; so, I do not drink. Drinking has only one benefit: it gives a headache. I smoke only on stage and screen. For any woman, smoking amounts to making herself cheap. Moreover, none of the cine-lovers has expressed any objection to my particularities. People these days are emotional. I have discovered what they want and I exactly ply with them. People say, and you have seen for yourself, that I have brought back the portrayal of real women on screen. And, that you can depend on Mae West's words; this has only been for the good.

Men judge women by their external attributes and according to their own whims. To speak the truth, men have never been able to overcome their inability to appreciate women comprehensively. I have thought about it calmly: why was there such a furor and disquiet in 1933 [at present]? It was because young men love physical beauty that stirs imagination. If you do not believe me, then you could call on the matrimonial offices for verification.

'I'M NO ANGEL'

The final courtroom sequence as played out in the film.[4]

The scene (Long Shot) opens in a courtroom brimming with people. The characters present in the scene are:

Ms Tira (Plaintiff)
Jack Clayton (Defendant)
Benny Pinkowitz (Tira's Attorney)
Bob (Clayton's Attorney)
Judge
Mr. Brown
Kirk Lawrence
Beulah Thorndyke (Tira's Maid)
Slick Wiley
Bailiff
Court officer
Members of the Jury
Photographers
Reporters
Courtroom crowd

Bob moves towards the stand where Tira is seated, and begins his interrogation. He digs into Tira's 'colourful past', making suggestions that she had always been overtly friendly towards men. Bob tries hard to pin her down, but Tira sails through the first scene unperturbed, being ruthlessly witty and candid about her friendship with men, and loudly claiming to know the men she was asked to identify by Bob.

Bob: Miss Tira, I understand you've had a rather colourful past.

Tira: I gotta admit I've been the love interest in more than one guy's life. I don't see what my past has got to do with my present.

She admitted she knew them all though could not recollect their names. Tira's defense lawyer, Benny, utterly dismayed by her actions, asks for a ten-minute-break.

Benny: Why didn't you tell me there were so many men in your life?

Tira: Why, shouldn't I know guys? I've been around. I travel from coast to coast. A dame like me can't make trips like that without meeting some of the male population.

Benny loses patience and sees no probability of turning the case in Tira's favour. So Tira decides to question the defence witnesses herself. When Bob takes the statement from Mr. Brown, one of the witnesses, the latter claimed that he met Tira at a dance show where she

Ms. Tira (Mae West) being questioned

flirted with him. Later, she lured him to her hotel room, they danced together and she kissed him during the act. Tira begins to cross-examine Mr. Brown after this statement. It becomes evident that Mr. Brown had married five times, and while he spent time with Tira he was still married to one of them. Tira rebuffed Mr. Brown, 'You made it sound nasty the way you spoke about us two being alone together in my place. And you know nothing actually happened that you couldn't tell your grandchildren about.'

> Mr. Brown: Well, I...
> Tira: In other words, it was just a harmless little social date, wasn't it?
> Mr. Brown: Yeah.
> Tira: Okay, I'm through with you.
> Tira (To the Juror): How am I doing?

Through her caustic comments and sharp wit Tira proves that Mr. Brown had presented the happenings in a different colour though in reality 'it was just a harmless little social date'. Mr. Brown has no option but to agree with Tira. Tira seems to be glad at her initial success. Further, the judge is seemingly charmed by Tira and asks the court to present the next witness on the stand.

Bob begins questioning Kirk Lawrence who happened to know Tira very closely, so much so that once he had even contemplated marrying her. It becomes evident from the interrogation that during their courtship, which probably lasted for a week, Kirk had presented her with expensive gifts such as a diamond bracelet, gowns, a fur coat, and so on. However, their relationship apparently broke at the time Tira became engaged to Mr. Clayton, who was financially stronger than Kirk. When Bob asks Kirk how he thinks Tira treated him in this whole affair, Kirk accuses Tira of having used him to get something better. When it comes to Tira's turn to question Kirk, she begins bluntly: 'You're not looking to get those presents back, are you, Mr. Lawrence?' She clarifies further,

Ms. Tira (Mae West) impresses the judge

'You gave me those presents because you liked me a little, didn't you?' And, 'I didn't ask you for them, did I?'

Kirk defends himself reiterating that he had no regrets ever for having presented her with those gifts. So Tira brings out the actual picture, pointing out forthright, 'Now, you were engaged to marry a girl just at the time you started running around with me, wasn't you? ...And you know your fiancée came up to me to see me to ask me to break it off with you, don't you? ...All right, I broke it off. So what are you crying about?'

The juror burst out in laughter. Bob summons his next witness Beulah Thorndyke, Tira's personal maid.

Tira, utterly surprised, comments, 'You don't have to tell me they had nerve enough to call my own maid to squeal on me?'

Though Bob tries to make an assertion that even after Tira was engaged with Mr. Clayton she entertained other male visitors at home, which Beulah denied. So Bob gets frustrated and accuses Beulah of having a 'convenient memory'. Following this, Tira proceeds with her questions, but first, asks Beulah to explain why she had been called.

'I don't know Ma'm. They done subpoenaed me,' she replies. Tira requests her to tell 'the boys the truth'.

Tira clarifies through Beulah's answers that after getting engaged with Mr. Clayton, she had not talked about any other man nor was she visited by any other man, except her manager, Mr. Barton. She asks Beulah if she ever heard her talking or joking about Mr. Clayton's wealth. Finally, she asks Beulah, 'Did you hear me say what I thought about Mr. Clayton?' And directs her to turn towards the jury and explain. Beulah bursts out emphatically, 'You said that you never knew you could love a man like you love him.' Tira retorts, 'I kind of forgot I said that.' Undeterred Beulah continues, 'And you said you had fallen so hard for him

The case turns on Ms. Tira's (Mae West) side

that it hurt.' Tira seems to be a bit taken aback and rebuffs, 'Wait a minute. Answer one question at a time.'

Beulah clarifies that she was merely telling the truth as was requested. Tira wittily remarks, 'Yes, but you're telling too much of it.'

Beulah, overwhelmed to express her loyalty towards Tira, continues, 'I ain't never seen nobody so brokenhearted as you was when you and Mr. Clayton done bust up.' Tira, comments sarcistically, 'That's enough, Beulah. You're ruining my character.'

The last witness asked to take the stand is Slick Wiley. Though Jack Clayton asks his attorney Bob if it was necessary to summon him, Bob emphasizes that he was depending on his statements as he was sure that Tira will not be able to 'laugh him off'. However, Jack warns Bob not to mention about the night when he found Jack in her apartment, to which Bob clarifies that he must raise the issue to pin down Tira, though he would keep it 'as clean as possible'. Benny becomes a bit nervous and warns Tira that Slick's statements may prove to be the deciding factor for the case.

Through the interrogation, Slick projects that he was a regular visitor to Tira's house, more than a friend to her, and he continued visiting her even after she was engaged to Mr. Clayton. She also paid him handsome amounts regularly. She allowed him to keep his personal belongings at her house, which also included two pyjamas, one green and the other purple with yellow stripes. She had even confided to him that she was interested in Mr. Clayton because of his wealth. At this point Bob leaves Slick to be cross-examined by Tira.

Tira begins directly, 'Where were you on the night of June 7?' When Slick says he does not remember, Tira asks bluntly, 'All right, I'll give you a choice, where were you any night last June, July, or August? Come on, make up your mind.'

Tira has put Slick in a very uncomfortable position by raising this question, and Slick replies, 'In stir'.

Tira clarifies, 'He was in stir. That means, in other words, gentlemen of the jury, he was in jail. Tell the gentlemen how many other jails you've been in the last 10 years.'

When Slick denies, Tira pins him down further: 'He can't remember. And what's this about you owning silk pyjamas? You know it's a lie. You forgot to tell these good people the only time I ever gave you money was when you got out of jail, you were broke, and walking on your heels. ... As for you sitting in my apartment in silk pyjamas you never sat around my apartment in nothing. And you know it. Answer me, did you?'

Slick refuses to give way and replies, 'Sure, I did. And I was seen there, too.'

Tira enraged by Slick's lies calls him a perjuror, to which Bob raises his objection to the witness being harassed by such accusations. Tira bursts out saying, 'Who's harassing who? I'm just asking for a square deal, that's all. I'm asking good, honest and intelligent people not to take the word of an ex-convict against a good, honest and innocent woman.'

Despite Bob raising objection to Tira's pleadings, it gets overruled and he concludes, '... She's got the jury and the judge

Ms. Tira (Mae West) wins through her wit and ingenuity

under her arm. They'll hand her the case on a silver platter.' Jack intervenes, saying that such a claim by Bob is unfair on Tira. Bob infuriated retorting back, 'Unfair? Maybe you've got so much money, you don't mind losing this case. But my reputation means something to me. If ever there was a case I wanted to win, this is it.'

Jack reminds Bob that he had asked him not to summon Slick but Bob had insisted. Bob points out that now it was time for Jack to take the stand to present the entire story before the court. Jack refuses to participate, which increases Bob's frustration. He asks Jack, 'If you feel that way about it, why did you contest the case at all?' Jack simply says, 'Well, I'm sorry I did.'

Tira takes the opportunity to present a conclusive decision before the jurors, saying, 'If any right-thinking man will believe what a crook and a jailbird will say then there's nothing I could say that'll make any difference. I'm through with this guy, Judge.'

Though Bob tries to fight back and questions Slick again, Jack steps back and even offers to pay for the damages to close the case. Bob has no option but to appeal before the judge to close the case.

The judge announces, 'In view of the agreement between the parties the jury is discharged with thanks. Case dismissed. Court's adjourned.'

Tira is surprised at the outcome. She is flanked by reporters and photographers. One of the reporters asks if she is willing to answer a few questions. A jubilant Tira heeds to their request. Here is a brief extract:

Reporter 2: You've won the case. What do you intend to do?
Tira: Carry on the same as before.
Female Reporter: Why did you admit knowing so many men in your life?
Tira: It's not the men in your life that counts, it's the life in your men.
Reporter 3: In all this do you feel you've done right?
Tira: Show me a woman who can do better. FADE OUT

NOTES

1 Published in *Journal of Arts and Ideas*, 2 January–March 1983.
2 Meena Kumari's poems have been translated by Madhuja Mukherjee.
3 A translated article of Mae West's open letter appeared in *Chitrapanji* (4)4, January–February 1934: 202–204. The article, presented in this volume, is translated from the Bengali article that appeared in *Chitrapanji* by Atig Ghosh.
4 Mae West wrote the screenplay of *I'm No Angel* (1933: Dir Weslet Ruggles). A description of the final courtroom scene with a few intercepting lines from the screenplay throw light on her caustic tone, her 'quotable quotes' and her wit.

WOMEN CONCEIVING CINEMA: TALKING STARS

4

The first attempts to discuss issues pertaining to the industrial aspect of Indian cinemas came up with the 1927–28 Indian Cinematograph Committee Report (commissioned by the Empire). The Cinematograph Committee was devised to validate the aspiration to control the production and exhibition of films made by Indians, just as it hoped to encourage the growth of British films. The Committee (comprising three Indians and three Englishmen) examined the effectiveness of the industry, while the questions addressed to respectable subjects of the country hovered around production and exhibition conditions, the efficiency of the Indian filmmakers, moral issues and an ambiguous argument about quality films. Members of the legislative committee, police officers, judges, professors, political leaders, actors, producers, filmmakers, and others were interviewed. Issues of censorship, control over exhibition sectors, economy of production and gender questions recur in all interviews. However, contrary to the expectations, the Committee rejected the proposal to give preferential treatment to British films; instead, it demanded a programme to support Indian producers. The

All Quiet on the Western Front *(1930) was a hit at New Theatres' flagship theatre Chitra in 1931*

Committee recommended that Indian producers should be able to take loans from public funds (though the English Committee members disapproved of this) and exhibition conditions should improve. It also suggested that a new department should come up with functions ranging from training to technical maintenance to organizing competitions for production and screenplay writing. Moreover, as far as the subject of 'good' cinema was concerned, western films were accepted, though censorship was encouraged. The report also proposed that cinema should be used as a means of mass education. Moreover, what emerged from these interviews was an intention to connect the technology of cinema with larger debates on Indian modernity, and examine the possibilities of cinema becoming the bearer of the emergent national modern. The moral overtones through which popular cinema and the 'problem of respectable ladies joining films' may be judged clearly got a definite shape through the ICC queries.[1]

Ruby Myers née Sulochana began her career with Kohinoor Film Company, Bombay. Later she shifted to Imperial Film Company where she became the highest paid star in India. Among her popular films were *Typist Girl* (1926), *Balidaan* (1927) and *Wildcat of Bombay* (1927) where she performed eight roles including male characters. During her peak (1928–29), she did extremely successful

Ruby Myers, in the magazine Filmland

films like *Madhuri* (1928), *Anarkali* (1928) and *Indira B.A.* (1929). With the advent of sound, she did not work for a while, and returned in 1932 with *Madhuri*. Curiously, she acted in the remakes of her own silent hits like *Bombay ki Billi* (1936). She was regularly paired with D. Billimoria and worked with him between 1933 and 1939. While Kaushik Bhaumik shows in his article the ways in which she figures as the glorious star and the iconic modern woman,[2] Neepa Majumdar illustrates how her star image underwent transformation and was reduced to a more demure one.[3] While Majumdar does remarkable research on early stardom, this volume, brings together writings pertaining to the issues of labour, work and gender within the context of the film as industry.[4]

INDIAN CINEMATOGRAPH COMMITTEE INTERVIEWS (1927–28) RUBY MYERS NÉE SULOCHANA

Oral Evidence of Miss RUBY MYERS, Actress, Imperial Film Co., [Bombay] on Saturday, the 12 November 1927.[5]

Chairman [icc]: Miss Myers, you have not favoured us with any written statement.
A. No.
Q. How long have you been in the profession?
A. Two years.
Q. And had you any training before you entered the profession?
A. No, I had no training.
Q. What were you doing before you entered the profession–if you don't mind my putting the question?
A. I was in the telephone office.
Q. Do you think it will be an advantage if we had some institution where training could be given to actors and actresses?
A. I think it would be a very good thing.

Q. Do you think there are many girls in Bombay who would be willing to come forward? You are fairly familiar with Bombay?
A. Very familiar.
Q. [Do] You come in contact with quite a number of girls of [sic] respectable Indian families?
A. Yes.
Q. Do you consider that, if a training class were opened, respectable girls and boys belonging to respectable families would join the profession?
A. Well, they would, if the cinema industry would rise.
Q. I suppose the cinema industry in the country is becoming more and more popular?
A. Yes.
Q. Not only foreign films but also Indian films?
A. Yes.
Q. And I understand from witnesses who have come before us that the Indian films are getting more and more popular with the Indian public?
A. Quite so.
Q. And what do you think should be done to make it more attractive?
A. Well, I think if we were financed properly ...
(The remainder of Miss Myers evidence was taken in camera.)

The Oral Evidence (taken in camera) of Miss Ruby Myers

Chairman: And what do you think should be done to make it [film-acting] more attractive?[6]
A. Well, I think if we were financed properly, if there were some technical improvements and if there were some way of getting fairly good stories—if we could get stories like Tagore's and some others, which I know would appeal to the educated classes—our stories at present are very poor. We want better stories, either taken from the ancient books or good modern authors.[7]

Women Conceiving Cinema: Talking Stars

Q. You want more literary effort in that direction?

A. Yes. And, of course, the studios are quite good in the present conditions. That is, things being what they are, they are quite good.

Q. Although you would like to have them improved, you would not insist on it at the present stage? What I want to know really is whether for the educated classes and also for girls of good family the conditions in the studios are sufficiently attractive. ...

A. Well, what I see of them they are very respectable company. They behave very well and they work very well.[8]

Q. Although they may have come from the lower class?

A. I don't think they have come from a very low class. Most of them are very very good company.

Q. I mean taking things as they are, there is not much room for complaint? You are fairly satisfied with [the] conditions in the studios?

A. Fairly. I have worked in three so far.

Q. And you don't think there is anything to take exceptions to?

A. I mean, there may be one or two things which may be improved, but really the conditions of life are not bad.

Q. I am glad to hear that. And what about the pay?

A. Well, I think for this kind of work the pay is very good. If, of course, the pictures bring in more money, I am sure the producers would be very willing to help us.

Q. So there is nothing to complain of in that direction?

A. No we are quite satisfied, I think that the stars and all the actors are quite satisfied with what they get.

Q. But will it improve matters if there are good story writers?

A. Yes.

Q. And what about technique?

A. Well, the story writers do not know the technique for the film. They just write the story out and it is the director who helps to make the scenario.

Q. Would it be an advantage if girls like you were given a six months' course or one year's course of training in England?

A. It would be a great advantage for us; and even for the actors I think, because we lack in [good] actors more [*sic*].

Q. Now you learn your art more from seeing the screen?

A. Yes, from studying the western pictures [films produced in the West or American and European films]. Of course, it has been my ambition from my childhood to become a film star. The first opportunity I got to enter the profession I availed myself of.

Q. And I suppose there must be several such people who, if given an opportunity, would be willing to do it?

A. I receive many letters from up-country asking to join...whether it is good for them to join, from students and others.

Q. From what class?

A. Well, from their letters [it seems] they must be [hailing from] a very good class. From Muhammadans [Muslims] mostly, and I have had one or two Anglo-Indian girls who wanted to join.

Q. From the actors and actresses' point of view, do you think any class here for training would be well attended? You must have very good experts to teach. Do you think you can get the experts?

A. I think at present it would be [a] waste of time. Because at present there are very few people who know about this art. What I find is that the few directors alone know about it.

Q. You mean you cannot get trained people here?

A. No. I have never come across anybody who could give the training.

Q. So you think it would be a good plan to send for a good trainer here, to be loaned to [to be hired by] the producing companies?

A. I think it would be a good thing.

Q. Do you think that these places where Indian films are produced should be licensed or should come under any system of issuing a license for opening studios?

Mr. Neogy [ICC member, referring to the Chairman]: Please explain the purposes for which you suggest it to be done.

Chairman: To see that the conditions of living are all right. In the city where there are studios, do you think they should be licensed at all?

A. I do not think so.

Q. Now, of course, that is a matter which we must put to politicians. I don't want to trouble you with a political question. Is there anything else you want to bring to the notice of the company? You know the objects [objectives] of this committee. Do you think there is anything which you would like to place before the committee?

A. No. I have nothing else to say.

Sir Haroon Jaffer [ICC member]: These people, the directors and proprietors and producers don't want to give out the secrets of their trade to anyone else at present. They are anxious to keep it to themselves and therefore they don't want to train anybody except their own people.

A. I don't know very much about that. On the contrary, I think they would help others to train.

Q. Would they like other companies started against them?

A. No.

Q. I want to know whether we should wait for the people to train themselves or whether you want [the] government to help the trade to produce better pictures.[9]

A. Well, I think we are quite all right.

Q. You don't want an up-to-date studio started by [the] government for the use of these producers and others? You don't like the idea?

A. No.

Q. There is an impression now that whatever [*sic*] actresses are in the studio at present are from an undesirable class. Is that right?

A. No I don't think so because most of them are very respectable and don't behave like that in company.

Q. What pay do you get yourself?

A. Rs 750, with a car.

Q. Is it a good pay?

A. I think so. It is quite a good pay. It would be increased if the pictures went well. It depends on the pictures.

Q. If you are sent, you would like to go and be trained? [Perhaps] a trip to England?

A. Well, I would only like to be trained for the benefit of the Indian industry.

Q. Of course, you would then come back and help the industry here.

A. That I would not mind.

Mr. Coalman [ICC member]: I think you said, Miss Myers, that you have been in this employment about two years?

A. Yes.

Q. Have you been with the same producing company the whole time?

A. No. I was one year with the Kohinoor. And I worked a picture for the Orient; the rest of the time I have been with the Imperial.

Q. You have had no difficulty in getting employment?

A. No, I find [*sic*] no difficulty.

Q. Had you any difficulty, in the first place, in getting employment?

A. You see I was working in the telephone company when my photographer happened to see my photograph and I think he had a play made for me which was my first play and he thought I could do something. He asked me and I got my opportunity.[10]

Q. Have you acted in play with other actresses?

A. Yes, I have acted with one of the stars of the Kohinoor, Miss Gohur.

Q. You have acted with European actresses and Indian actresses—both?

A. No, not European. Only Indian. Except my picture 'The Telephone Girl' where we had a few English actresses—a nurse I think.

Q. And did they also like the work?

A. Yes.

Q. And these other actresses with whom you acted, who were they?

A. They were Indians.

Q. I mean these Indian ladies.

A. Well they were ladies of different castes—Hindus and Muhammadans. Of course, they were very respectable.

Q. Any of them married?

A. Most of them are married in the Kohinoor Company.

Q. You are in constant employment? You had no difficulty in finding employment?

A. No.

Q. Are there more calls made on you than you can cope with? I mean there is full [regular] employment for you?

A. Oh, yes.

Q. Would you say then that there is scope for more ladies in the profession here?

A. Yes, there are heaps [*sic*] of scope, if they would only come.

Q. Then there is scope for Anglo-Indian girls and European girls as well as Indian girls?

A. I do not think they would be able to do the Indian girl.[11] It was a bit hard for me at first. I have been so much with Indians that I seem to get their habits and behaviour.

Q. You mentioned a film 'The Telephone Girl'. Was that an Indian film?

A. It was Indian in a way. It was about an Anglo-Indian girl who ultimately turned out to be an Indian girl. It was meant to appeal to an Indian audience. And it did appeal to them.

Q. Have you acted in any plays that were meant to appeal to European audiences?

A. No. I don't think so, except 'Sacrifice'.

Q. Well, you say there is scope for more actresses, but I take it those actresses must be Indian actresses. [You mean] there is scope for Indian actresses.

A. Yes.

Q. Then for future Indian actors, do you think a training institution would be a good thing?

A. Well, if they got any artistic instinct in them, if they can work, there is no need for it.

Chairman: Have you seen 'Savitri' screened here?

A. No.

Mr. Neogy: Had [Did] you [have] any experience of acting on the stage before you came to your present profession?
A. Not [*sic*], except for my school days.
Q. There is a good deal of difference between acting on the stage and acting on [*sic*] the screen?
A. A very vast difference.
Q. But do you think that those who have been a success or rather those who have got a talent for acting on the stage have an initial advantage for the screen?
A. Yes, I think so. Because Mr. Kambatta was a very well-known stage actor who acted in 'Sacrifice' and he has done well. I expect at moments you can find out such movements.
Q. So you think that the present stage furnishes a good training ground from that point of view for film actors and actresses?
A. I think it would, if they worked hard.
Chairman: But only today I saw a press cutting in one of the Bombay papers that the two things are totally different.
Mr. Neogy: True. She admits it. But they are allied, and those who have a liking for the stage could more easily take to the screen.
A. It would be hard for them at first but they would succeed, if they were directed well.
Q. They would be in a better position than the people going directly to screen acting.
A. Yes, they would understand better.
Q. You said a lot of Anglo-Indian girls and others have made inquiries from you about this profession. Do you think it is really very difficult for an Anglo-Indian girl—I am not talking of the European for the time being—to adopt herself to Indian ways and interpret Indian ideas?
A. It is not very difficult if she has got the knack of walking and behaving like an Indian–just as I do.
Q. It is not an insuperable difficulty?
A. No.
Q. We are told that there is an Anglo-Indian girl who has made a great success of a film in Calcutta?
A. I have not seen her act.

Colonel Crawford [ICC member]: Miss Myers, I want to examine you from the point of view of the actors and actresses only. Are you satisfied that there is a sufficiency of material to make suitable actors and actresses in India?
A. I think so.

Q. You are getting a sufficiency of proper people at present?
A. Well, I think so. I have had that experience and I have done well in it.

Q. You think there are plenty of actors and actresses available?
A. I think so.

Q. You have given me the idea that the subjects of the films and technique are not good enough at present for the expansion of the industry. With your present personnel, are the actors and actresses up to the work of producing better films?[12]
A. Most of them I think are.

Q. Undoubtedly, individuals would be, but do you think the majority would be?
A. Most of them would be. If they had a good story, I think most of them would work for it.

Q. Sufficiently to be attractive abroad?[13]
A. Yes, if the director is there and producer spends the money, I don't see why we can't do it.

Q. And are there any comic actors available?
A. Yes, we have them.

Q. I have not seen a comic Indian scene, not the type of Harold Lloyd.
A. Oh, no.

Q. Well, now what are the conditions under which you work at present? You contract for whole-time work for certain producing companies?
A. Well, this is the first time I have made a contract. As a rule I never make contracts.

Q. You prefer to make contracts for a particular picture?
A. No. I don't [make a contract] for a particular picture. Lately I have made it for six months or for six pictures.

Q. And you are open after that to take on a contract anywhere you like?

A. Oh, yes.

Q. But you are satisfied that you yourself have a chance to make your own conditions wherever you like? Under [the] existing conditions, you can [draw a] contract where you like and for any picture you like?

A. [Yes] The moment my work finishes.

Q. The terms of the contract you don't consider are disadvantageous from the actor's point of view. Can you give me an idea of the salaries of actors?

A. I know one actress who gets Rs 1,200 a month. Some get a thousand. Some of them have been four or five years in service.[14]

Q. Those are your stars. But what does a beginner get?

A. It all depends. To tell you the truth, I don't know how others have begun, but for me, I began on Rs 150 and when the producer saw that I could work for my first picture he gave me a rise of another Rs 100 on his own account and in two years I have risen to Rs 750.

Q. You think, as far as salaries are concerned, that [*sic*] educated people would be able to get salaries that would attract them?

A. Yes, if the company could afford to pay them.

Q. Now you are getting down to it. That is rather the point I want to get at. Have Indian producers an opportunity to make good films?

A. They have the best opportunity. It is only the finances that they want.

Q. But can they get a return of money [*sic*] in India to pay these big salaries?

A. Well, if the picture goes well and the story is good, I don't see why they shouldn't.

Q. Do you think the type of films you are producing is rather a cheap [low budget] type?

A. Well, it appeals to the Indians very much.

Q. Quite well enough? There is no necessity to produce anything more expensive?

A. Well, no. If you make an expensive film or a cheap film, if they think the story is good they will like it.

Q. But what I want to get at is if the majority of the films produced by these companies today are what I would call the cheaper type of films?

A. Well, I know they spend lots of money on some films.

Q. But what is the proportion?

A. I think on one film they spent Rs 40,000. Of course, I have not pried into their private affairs.[15]

Q. I don't want to pry in any way. I just want to find out whether there is an opportunity for bigger salaries.

A. Yes, there is.

Mr. Green [ICC member]: I understand Miss Myers that you like the work. It interests you and you don't find it too hard?

A. Yes.

Q. You get fairly long hours?

A. Yes, if there is work you have to be working from 10 [a.m.] to 6 [p.m.]. Sometimes we work every day.

Q. I should try and get from you the elements that go to make a good actor or actress?

A. One must have a natural intelligence.

Q. I take it that if one had the advantage of a good education coupled with natural intelligence, it would be better?

A. Yes, quite so.

Q. You were educated in Bombay?

A. Yes.

Q. When you have got a good education and natural intelligence, I understand that a good director also has a lot to do in making the play a success?

A. Yes.

Q. You have told us that there is plenty of raw materials in the way of actors and actresses in the making among Indians [*sic*]?

A. Yes.

Q. But is it not a little bit difficult to induce Indian ladies to come forward and take part in theatres?

A. They are rather shy, but I think some of them are getting over it.

Q. What about education?

A. I know four or five of them have not had any education worth the name and yet they have sufficient intelligence and natural intelligence and do very well as actresses.

Q. Would that not apply to male actors as well?

A. Most of the male actors are not educated; only very few are educated, but if they had education they could act better. But we are quite satisfied with their present acting even though some of them are not educated.

Q. You think that the innate capacity of a man to act is more important when you say that some actors are not educated and yet they are really very good actors?

A. They do their work well.

Chairman: Most of the male actors you refer to, I suppose, behave well; is it not?

A. Yes.

Mr. Coalman: You know that in England and other countries people take to the theatrical profession merely for the love of acting. Have you met any people of that kind in this country. I mean people taking to the profession for the mere love it?

A. I have met some uneducated persons.

Q. I am thinking of the females?

A. It is very difficult for the European or Anglo-Indian girls to come into this profession. But some of the Indian ladies would do very well as they have got lovely long hair.[16]

Colonel Crawford: There are no difficulties in the way of getting actors and actresses?

A. No, none.

Q. Have you any suggestions to make so as to make the conditions better for the actors and actresses?

A. I have no suggestions to make.

Patience Cooper began her career at a very early age, and her first film *Nala Damayanti* was released in 1922. She acted in several Madan films, which were adaptations of Bankim Chandra Chattopadhyay's novels. These films were mostly screened in theatres like Cornwallis Theatre, Calcutta, and were not full-length feature films.

Patience Cooper

Sita Devi in Light of Asia

Sita (also **Seeta**) **Devi** or Rainey Smith too, as described here, joined Madan Theatres, the most influential production-distribution-exhibition company of the period, after her associations with Himanshu Rai's *Light of Asia* (Dir. Franz Osten, 1921) and other films. Her successful films included *Light of Asia, Shiraz,* and *Prapancha Pash* ('A Throw of Dice').

These films were produced by Himanshu Rai and his German collaborators. While the first film, was based on the life of Buddha, 'A Throw of Dice', was based on a story from the *Mahabharata*.

INDIAN CINEMATOGRAPH COMMITTEE INTERVIEWS (1927–28) PATIENCE COOPER AND RAINEY SMITH NÉE SITA DEVI

Oral Evidence of Miss Rainey Smith [Sita Devi in Light of Asia] and Miss Patience Cooper, Actresses

> **Miss Cooper:** I have been connected for nine years with the film industry even [*sic*] since this film production was started in Bengal.[17]
>
> Chairman: I suppose you have been acting only in Bengal?
> **A.** Yes.
> **Q.** Have you been to Bombay at all?
> **A.** No.
> **Q.** Miss Sitadevi [*sic*], how long have you been connected with this?
> **Miss Sita Devi:** For three years.
> **Q.** Both of you like the job?
> **A.** Yes.
> **Q.** Both of you act on the stage?
> **A.** [Sita Devi] No, only on the stage.
> **Q.** Miss Cooper, I thought you acted on the stage also?
> **Miss Cooper:** Just for the show of the Corinthian Theatre, not always.

Q. How many girls are there now in Bengal who appear on the film?

Miss Cooper: There are a number of girls now, but I do not know whether they are on the permanent list or not.

Q. How many girls take to it?

Miss Cooper: I think there are six others apart from Miss Sitadevi [*sic*].

Miss Sita Devi: I do not know of any one.

Q. Do you think that Bengali girls are likely to take to this profession?

Miss Cooper: We have got some Bengali girls in this film acting. They come and go off and on.

Q. But they do come?

A. Yes.

Q. None of them are taken on a permanent employment?

A. I do not think so.

Q. Do you know of any who is in permanent employment by any studio?

A. No.

Q. I suppose you always work with Madans?

A. Yes.

Miss Sita Devi: No, the first picture I was in was 'The Light of Asia'. That was my first picture. Later on I came to [the] Madans.[18]

Q. You are now with Madan's [*sic*]?

Miss Sita Devi: Yes.

Q. There were other ladies in 'The Light of Asia'. Do you know them at all?

A. Yes.

Q. Was it also their first time?

A. Yes.

Q. Now as regards the conditions of the studio life in this province, are the conditions suitable for people like you going in to the trade? Are you treated well by the male actors?[19]

A. Oh, yes.

Q. They are strangers; are you treated well?

A. Yes.

Q. You don't experience any trouble or nuisance?

A. No.

Q. Is that also your experience Miss Cooper?

Miss Cooper: Yes.

Q. How do you acquaint yourself with Indian ways when you appear as Indian ladies on the stage?

Miss Cooper: I have studied their ways. I have been with them for so many years, and the directors guide us.

Q. And you move with the people?

A. Yes.

Q. I suppose you have nothing in particular to say about the lady actresses who appear on the films which you think this Committee should take note of? Is there anything you wish to bring to the notice of this Committee?

A. No.

Q. You think the conditions are all right and the conditions are likely to attract good people to the screen. That is what we are anxious to know.

A. Oh, yes.

Q. You joined the business after you left school.

A. Yes.

Q. You were in school before that?

A. Yes.

Q. Why did you take to this?

Miss Sita Devi: It is very interesting

Q. Do you prefer Indian Companies?

A. There is no chance of going abroad or of joining any European companies [*sic*].

Q. I suppose if they employed you now you would like to go?

A. Oh, yes.

Q. At less remuneration or more?

A. More.

Q. Miss Cooper, you also came out of school and joined this business?

Miss Cooper: No, I first joined the stage after I left school— Bandman's Musical Comedy Company. I then left the Company and I was in Calcutta when Mr. Madan saw me dancing at some show and asked me to dance at his show.

He told me he was starting a producing [sic] company and I stayed on with him.[20]

Q. How much do you get now?

A. I would rather not say.

Q. Do you get good remuneration, can you say that?

A. No.

Sir Haroon Jaffer: You are pleased with it. You want more?

A. Yes.[21]

Chairman: As you like this profession, would you like to continue in it?

A. Yes.

Sir Haroon Jaffer: You mix with Indian ladies also in this cinema company?

A. We do work with them.

Q. How do you find them, are they of respectable family?

A. Away from the studio, I don't know them at all.

Q. You don't know their private life?

A. No.

Q. But when you meet them you think they come from respectable families?

A. Yes, they seem all right; they seem quite nice.

Q. I want to know about the respectability of their family. They behave all right in the studio?

A. They behave all right.

Mr. Neogy: Do you know Bengali?

A. No.

Q. When you have to interpret certain sentiments for the film you have to depend upon the directions given by the director?

A. Yes, he explains everything in English.

Q. You don't find it at all inconvenient to interpret those things?

A. No.

Mr. Coalman: I would just like to know how you came in the first place to take to the profession.

Chairman: She has told us already that she was on the stage.

Q. How old were you when you first began to act?

Miss Sita Devi: 13. In 'The Light of Asia'.

Q. And how did you get into it, did you answer an advertisement?

A. Yes.

Q. How were you chosen?

A. There were about 3,000 applicants. The Germans came out to produce 'The Light of Asia' and they put in an advertisement.[22]

Mr. Neogy: How many months did it take to produce that picture?

Sita Devi in Shiraz

A. Six months.

Chairman: Can you tell us of the 3,000 applications, how many were Bengalis or Anglo-Indians?

A. I heard from the Company that there were 3,000 applicants. I did not see them.

Q. Were you given an individual interview or did you appear with the others?

A. An individual interview. The Manager saw some of them every day.

Q. And who were the other people who applied? Were they all Anglo-Indians?

A. There were some English girls also.

Mr. Green: Indian girls also?

A. Mostly Anglo-Indians and Europeans.

Mr. Coalman: Miss Cooper is it your opinion that this profession of film actress will have to remain for the present, at any rate, in the hands of Anglo-Indian or European girls in India?

Miss Cooper: I don't know. The Indian girls do just as well even now.

Q. You have acted with Indian girls?

A. Yes.

Q. Were they educated girls?

A. I don't know. They seemed all right. I cannot say whether they were educated or not.

Chairman: She just sees them in the studio and does know them outside [the studio].

A. Some of them belong to the stage, the Bengali theatre. They joined the theatre when they were very young.[23]

Col. Crawford: Are you satisfied with the publicity you get Miss Cooper?

A. No.

Miss Sita Devi: I am quite satisfied. [....]

INDIAN CINEMATOGRAPH COMMITTEE INTERVIEWS (1927–28) PUNJAB BOARD OF FILM CENSORS

Oral Evidence, [Indian Cinematograph Committee Report (1927–28)] the Punjab [Province] Board of Film Censors on Thursday, the 24th November 1927

(1) Mr. J. E. Parkinson, M.A. Principal, Central Training College,
(2) Ms. M. Bose,
(3) Mrs. Shah Nawaz,
(4) Mr. H. W. Webb,
(5) Khan Bahadur Nawab Muzaffar Khan, Director of the Information Bureau and Secretary of the Board.[24]

[....] **Q.** I suppose you are interested in the cinema? You go to the cinema although your board was only recently started.

Miss Bose: I certainly don't go to the cinema unless it is something very special.

Q. None of you have interested yourself in the subject so as to be able to tell us whether there is a possibility for the industry in this province? What are the potentialities?

Mrs. Shah Nawaz: I think there is a possibility. There is a growing need which has been felt by most of the educated people that they should have films which would tell them of their historical events.[25]

Q. You think the Indian public want them?

A. I think they do. [....]

Chairman: You think at any rate, so far as instructional films are concerned, whether it be propaganda, public health, modern methods of agriculture, or general subjects for the education and instruction of the people, and topical ... .

Mrs. Shah Nawaz: It is one of the best means of propaganda.

Q. Now what is your considered opinion on the point? You think the government should undertake the production of such films or do you think if it is left to the private agency [*sic*], they would be able to do it?

Mr. Parkinson: Personally, I would not give an opinion on that because I have not come to any conclusion.

Mrs. Shah Nawaz: But government should give monopolies to certain companies.

Chairman: I should like you to think over it. Because it won't pay private agencies to produce such educational films.[26]

Mr. Green: You have just told us you could not get the films.

Chairman: It won't be an attractive proposition commercially to them, although they may be induced to exhibit a certain length along with their programme. But this is more the function of Government than of a private agency, isn't it?

Mrs. Shah Nawaz: We have to think of it carefully, because money is needed in this country for so many things.

Q. Quite true, but this is a question of the instruction of the people.

Mrs. Shah Nawaz: Yes. In connection with health propaganda and also morals we could have films made with the funds at our disposal.

Q. But apart from this, you think that it is essential that it should be undertaken?

A. Oh yes.

Q. Of course, if private agencies are forthcoming, so much the better. Do you think private agencies will be forthcoming in any reasonably short time in this province? [...]

Mr. Parkinson: I raised the question with members of my staff who are in a better position to judge than I am and without exception they told me that the usual films shown—I mean the American drama film—is [*sic*] decidedly harmful. Their reason was that the majority of the audience regard the scenes shown in the cinema as being typical of western civilisation, that the people were not sufficiently educated to understand the spirit in which the film is produced.

Q. That is the objection. Any other objection?

A. That was the only objection.

Miss Bose: The ladies are very much against the scenes shown. I asked them their opinion and they all cried it down. When I spoke to them about educational films they all said, 'Oh, yes, we like them, but we do not like the standard pictures that are shown to our children and we do not allow them to go.'

Q. But surely the cinema is an amusement, people go there for amusement, and if you are going to make it merely an educational factor, people ...

Miss Bose: They are certainly conservative ladies. They say it becomes a very exciting thing for the children, and if they go to such things over and over again nothing will keep them away from them, and my pandit told me they go so far as to steal money from their parents.

Q. People are going in large numbers?

A. Yes.

Q. Both men and women?

A. Many women go too now.

Q. So that I mean [*sic*] it is a relaxation to them. They go after a hard day's work for relaxation.

A. Some of the pictures are not at all good for boys and girls. The pictures of western life they see—they think it is all very bad and it brings the western people down in their estimation. It is very sad that they should have a very poor idea of England and America.[27]

Mr. Parkinson: Relaxation? It is an excitement among the student community.

Q. Supposing you do not show the pictures which you have in mind, do you think that the cinema will attract adults?

A. Possibly not.

Q. Either you will close down the cinema or censor the film in the way in which you want to ...

A. Or try to develop a better type of picture.

Q. You do not mind my putting a few questions? Is the Indian mind satisfied with what it sees in actual life among the Europeans? Do you think they understand it, say your short skirts, and other things?

A. Probably not. But you do not find a man kissing in the street.

Q. Probably you have a passing kiss.

A. It is not a passing kiss on the screen.

Q. What is the remedy? Is not education the proper remedy? Do you think that shutting the eyes of people and keeping them in the dark will help? Is it the proper remedy for that?

A. I think so, for the present.

Q. How long will you do that?

A. Until education has created a better public opinion. It is a matter of education.

Q. Don't you think the more they come to know it, the more will they give it a stage value and not consider it real? Do you think they really care to think about what they have seen when they have gone home? Do you think they really keep it in mind?

Miss Bose: They do [...]

Q. So that it is not a question of the so-called uneducated classes but of the youth?

A. And the knowledge behind.

Mrs. Shah Nawaz: If it is a question of the youth why not show them the other side and let them see what they will see later on life?

Miss Bose: Why should you bring these things into prominence?

Q. So long as you have the West with you, how can you hide it? Supposing young people go to England would you prevent them from going to the pictures?

Miss Bose: They are not illiterate people nor do they belong to the masses.

Q. Is it the young or the illiterate you have in mind?

Miss Bose: Both.

Q. Is it a very difficult problem for us. On one side you will kill the industry if you do not make it attractive, and on the other hand you have the possibility of injury to the public. The only thing you mentioned, Mr. Parkinson, was the possibility of the Westerner being misjudged. You did not say it has a demoralising effect. I asked you whether there was any other reason mentioned and you told me no. There is no question of demoralisation of the Indian public?

Mr. Parkinson: I certainly think if you are showing vice and passionate scenes it should have a demoralising effect.

Q. Then it has a demoralising effect also?

A. Yes.

Q. So that is another ground on which you object?

A. It is the same thing, it is only another aspect.

Q. It is not the same thing.

A. I regard the impression he gets about our civilization as demoralising for the Indian mind.

Q. Simply because you think that the westerner leads a fast life, how does it demoralise you?

A. Vices constantly shown to you make an impression on you.

Mr. Green: Is it a question of an eastern film or a western film? Would not an eastern film just as well have a demoralising effect?

A. It could. We do not see them.

Chairman: Can you give us any instances in your experience where youths have been led astray by going to the cinema?

Miss Bose: From crime scenes.

Q. I will come to that. I am now on the demoralising effect on the youth.

Mrs. Shah Nawaz: There is demoralising effect as well as moralising if I may say so.

Miss Bose: It all depends upon the film.

Q. You have not seen the films yourself?

Miss Bose: I have not.

Q. You are not in a position to tell us about it?

Miss Bose: No.

Q. Can you give us any instance of a film which you think is objectionable in that way?

Women Conceiving Cinema: Talking Stars

Mr. Parkinson: I can give you one instance where a cinema film has led to wrongdoing, a bicycle was stolen ...

Khan Bahadur Nawaz Muzaffar Khan: That was where an accused said he got it from the cinema. It was criminally suggestive.

Q. What we are after is this, whether the effect of the cinema is such as to call for any drastic action on the part of [the] government?

Mr. Parkinson: I should say not to my knowledge.

Q. These generalisations are made and when you come to particulars you always find it difficult. Can you, for instance, tell us of any film which you have seen, which you thought was objectionable and ought not to have been passed?

A. In 'The Sheik' I object to the Sheik carrying the woman away bodily.

Mrs. Shah Nawaz: Some scenes in 'Ki-Ki' were very objectionable—about the slums of Paris.

Q. We have information from the police both in Bombay and here that so far as crime is concerned they cannot say there is any development of crime in consequence of the cinema. You alluded to the case of a boy stealing a bicycle?

Mr. Parkinson: Yes.

Q. How do you connect it with the cinema?

A. He said he learnt the method of stealing the bicycle from the cinema.

Mr. Green: Is that a very common plea in other countries and in this country on the part of the accused in the hope of extenuating the punishment?

A. Yes.

Q. How long ago was that?

A. I cannot tell you.

Chairman: Would you rather have an injury to the trade or have what you consider educative, instructive and moralising films shown?

A. There is only one answer to that. I am sorry for the trade, but as I say it would not break the trade.

Q. I suppose a little more careful censorship is all that you want?

All: Yes.

Q. That is what you are aiming at, not that the injury is so great as to call for any drastic action. Do I understand you aright [*sic*]?

Mrs. Shah Nawaz: There is a great need of good films.

Q. The real remedy is the production of good films.

Mrs. Shah Nawaz: In order to educate the public mind.

Miss Bose: Indian films would appeal more to them because they will understand them better.

Q. The remedy lies in better production and a little more care in censorship?

Miss Bose: Yes.

Q. We are all human and human censorship boards are likely to err.

Mr. Webb: More sporting films [films about sports] ought to be produced.

Mr. Green: Are you referring to films produced in India or generally?

Mrs. Shah Nawaz: We are talking generally of films?

Mr. Webb [ICC member]: Produced in India. For instance, if you have a picture of race meetings, steeplechases, polo tournaments, hockey tournaments and the like I think they will be very attractive and they do no harm. As a matter [of] fact, the northern India men are very good sportsmen and they take in a large numbers to these races, polo tournaments and so on.

Chairman: Supposing we were to produce Indian films either by direct effort or by indirect effort of the kind you have in mind, would you make it obligatory on each cinema to show a certain proportion of Indian films?

Mr. Parkinson: I would.

Q. You know that they sometimes complain that their usual clientele would drop in numbers if they show Indian films.

Mrs. Shah Nawaz: If they showed a good deal.

Q. But if a little portion of each show consisted of Indian films it would be an encouragement to the industry?

Mr. Webb: A film showing the best polo champion would attract tremendously. If the film is not very long and if you have short lengths it will help a great deal.

Q. Short lengths can be introduced. You have no objection to making it compulsory on each cinema to show a certain length of Indian films provided it is not too long?
Mr. Webb: No.

Colonel Crawford: I should like to deal with you in your capacity of censors. You have stated that you consider a little closer censorship is necessary. Can you give me any particular idea of the nature of your objections, what the censor has got to do and what portion he has to cut out and so on?

Mr. Parkinson: We have exactly that difficulty amongst us. There was one film that was produced here on cooperation and usury and the injurious effects of usury. The money-lender was a Hindu and one of the gentlemen strongly objected to that being shown as it would arouse ill feeling between the Hindus and the Mussalmans. I see no point in that at all. I pass it, but a colleague of mine would not.

Q. Is there any point on which you think you are generally agreed?

A. We are generally agreed on what are called passionate love scenes and the like.

Q. I take it you will agree that close-up scenes of kissing might well be curtailed?

A. Yes.

Q. That is one definite point on which you agreed?

A. Yes.

Q. What about scenes of debauchery which occasionally come in?

A. Those I would cut out a great deal.

Chairman: Have you seen any scenes of debauchery on a film?

A. I have distinct recollection of one or two, but I cannot remember what portion was cut off.

Q. If there were scenes of debauchery I am sure the Censorship Board would have censored them themselves.

A. I will cut out all scenes where naked women are shown.

Q. Even if it is a work [of] art?

A. Yes.

Miss Bose: No.

Colonel Crawford: Have you seen any such films [*sic*]?

Mr. Parkinson: Generally speaking, I should cut out all passionate love scenes and scenes of debauchery. There was a film named 'Orphans of the Storm' which had very objectionable scenes.

Q. Is it being publicly exhibited?

A. It was stopped.

Q. The film was censored at Bombay?

Inspector: Yes.

Mr. Coalman: It has been entirely banned?

Inspector: Yes in the Punjab.

Q. From your point of view it might still be cut a little further?

Mr. Parkinson: Not so much from the point of view of the Board but from the point of view, in my opinion, of the value given to mob rule.

Mrs. Shah Nawaz: But that is in many other films and worse things too. I really see no reason why this film should not be passed.

Khan Bahadur Nawaz Muzaffar Khan: We have not yet decided it. It is still pending before the Board.

Colonel Crawford: Have you seen any Indian films shown in the Punjab yet?

Mr. Parkinson: Not one.

Q. Has any member of the Board seen an Indian film?

Khan Bahadur Nawaz Muzaffar Khan: The Punjab prepared films I have seen.

Q. They are mostly of an educational character?

A. Yes.

Mrs. Shah Nawaz: I have seen the 'Light of Asia'.[28]

Q. You have seen none of the films which are now produced in Bombay?

Khan Bahadur Nawaz Muzaffar Khan: No. I saw one in Bombay two years ago prepared [made], probably, by the Municipal Committee showing the effects of early marriage and so on.

Mrs. Shah Nawaz: I think 'The Light of Asia' was produced in Bombay.

Mr. Green: It was not purely an Indian film; it was prepared with foreign co-operation.

Mr. Neogy: The actors and actresses were all Indians.

Colonel Crawford: Have you any suggestions to make regarding captions? Do you think that the western serials will be understood better if you have options in Urdu as well as English?

A. That would make the film very long because in the Punjab, Urdu is not the only language. We have got Hindi, Gurumukhi and so on.

Q. We have seen four different languages on the screen. They are all shown at the same time.

Mrs. Shah Nawaz: If they are shown at the same time it won't make the film long.

Q. You have seen a certain number of Indian [*sic*] produced films in the Punjab?

Inspector: Yes.

Q. Can you give us any idea of their popularity with the audience?

A. Yes. Sometimes there is trouble. Lately there was a film called *Nur Jehan*. It was shown in one theatre on McLeod Road and when it was taken to the city they objected to it. We had to stop it because it would cause trouble between the two communities.

Chairman: You mean the audience objected to it?

A. One caste says it is objectionable and the other caste says it is not and thus it causes a lot of friction between the two communities.

Mr. Webb: About 'Nur Jehan' I asked some Muhammadans who told me that the objection entertained was not justified. I think sometimes it is probably due to jealousy between one firm and another.

Mr. Neogy: Have you seen the film?

Mrs. Shah Nawaz: No.

Colonel Crawford: The object of your Board is to censor local productions. You do not worry very much about western films?

Khan Bahadur Nawaz Muzaffer Khan: That is the main object, but still we are keeping in touch with all the shows. We have not taken any action so far, but we intend taking action regarding western films also.

Q. You will accept a certificate of the Board of Censors either in Bombay or Calcutta?

A. Yes, unless we think that there is a great deal of objection to it.

Q. How is your Board financed?

A. We have been given only Rs 500 for the expenditure, but I think to start with it is quite sufficient.

Q. Do you consider so far as the western films are concerned, it is necessary to have your own board in the province?

A. I think it is because, after all, India is a big continent and films which may be liked in Bombay or Calcutta may not be liked in the Punjab.

Q. Have you known very many cases of films having to be stopped in the Punjab?

A. One film that was stopped—we did not stop it but the Deputy Commissioner and the Punjab government stopped it—was 'Orphans of the Storm' and if we go a little further into the North-West Frontier Province it is likely to create more misunderstandings. We do not interfere in every film, but only whenever we find a certain film is likely to have a bad effect.

Q. My impression at the moment is that a very few of the films which pass through the Bengal or Bombay Board of Censors are objected to, it is a very, very small proportion.

A. Yes.

Q. And I would like to know your views whether you would not get greater uniformity by censoring the whole of the western films at one place?

A. If all the provinces are represented on that Board.

Q. Is there any particular necessity for each province to be represented on that Board in view of the fact that you are already accepting the censorship of Bombay or Bengal and there is at present only occasional objection to such films?

A. Some of these western scenes I would not like my Pathan neighbours to see because they would give a very low impression.

Q. Does the North-West Frontier Province come under your censorship?

A. No. My district is just on the border.

Q. What is your objection to showing these films to them?
A. It gives a very wrong impression and they are not very much educated.[29]

Mr. Neogy: What is the exact nature of the harm you fear?
A. It will produce a wrong impression.

Q. To whom will it be harmful?
A. I do not think it is in the interest of government either.

Q. The objection is on political grounds?
A. You might call it political.

Colonel Crawford: I would take [*sic*] you as regards the question of censoring western films. If each province is going to have its own board and judge each of these films, the boards might set up, and possibly will set up, a different standard for each province. Then what is going to be the position of the unfortunate man who imports these western films?
A. If each province or a group of one or two provinces is represented there then it will be all right.

Q. You do not think the sort of board which you get, for example, in a city like Bombay, is sufficient?
A. It is not sufficient. There is a great deal of difference.

Q. You already have a safeguard in that your district magistrate can suspend a film under the existing Act, and will that not be sufficient?
A. If that continues it is all right.

Q. Then Central Board with that safeguard will probably be adequate so far as western films are concerned?
A. Yes.

Q. Do you need your board for censoring your local production?
A. Yes.

Q. I notice here there are only 28 cinema theatres in the whole of the Punjab. 9 are in Lahore and 5 in Rawalpindi, and I presume the majority of the cinemas are in cantonments. Are there very many that are definitely catering for Indian audience?[30]

Inspector: There is one in the cantonment here and the others are in the civil area.

Q. Is an Indian film in the dress of another province likely to be appreciated here or should it be dressed in the dress of the province to be appreciated?

Khan Bahadur Nawaz Muzaffar Khan: Personally I think a Punjabi would prefer a film that is produced in the Punjabi dress.

Mrs. Shah Nawaz: But it is human nature to desire a change sometime and see the thing that others do. For instance, will not Bengalis like to see some local things of the Punjab just as we would like to see the things of Bengal? That would be a very good way also of making one province know what other provinces are like.

Mr. Green: Colonel Crawford has asked most of the questions I wanted to put. But as one who has been an ex-officio member of the Board of Censors in Bombay for some time, I am interested to know whether this Board has yet formed any general principles laying down what they consider objectionable and what they do not. I take it the Board is getting its experience at present.

A. Yes.

Mr. Parkinson: We have hardly begun to function yet. We have been in exercise a very short time and we have only had one meeting to find out what our powers are.[31]

Mrs. Shah Nawaz: The general impression in the country is that obscene scenes and scenes which lead to the breaking of the public peace should not be shown.

Q. Even 'obscene' is very hard to define?

Mrs. Shah Nawaz: It of course depends on one's point of view. It is very difficult for a Board to agree upon the point.

Q. The Board as a whole does not see films unless the officer who inspects them is doubtful of their propriety.

Khan Bahadur Nawaz Muzaffar Khan: That is so.

Q. Who actually inspects the films?

A. The Inspector of Police. He is a paid official. He has been doing that work for some time in Lahore.

Q. Is he a whole time servant of the Board?

A. He has nothing to do with the Board. He is employed by the Deputy Commissioner and the Superintendent of Police. He was on that duty before and we requested the

Deputy Commissioner, as we have not got sufficient funds, to let the arrangement continue for the present.

Q. At present you do not pay for that officer?

A. For the present we don't pay.

Q. As Secretary [Mr. Khan Bahadur Nawaz] do you receive any remuneration?

A. No.

Q. And none of the Board receives any remuneration?

A. No.

Q. You hope to build up a fund out of the fees you will charge?

A. I don't think there will be much income from that.

Q. Has the Board realised the difficulty that I think all censors have felt, that if you cut out everything, either from a western or an eastern film, to which someone might take objection there will be practically nothing left?

Ladies: Oh yes.

Q. I take it that is a difficulty you have felt and you are still trying to find a solution?

A. Yes.

Mr. Neogy: I find from the rules under the Cinematograph Act [1918] under which your Board has been constituted, that the Secretary is required to examine every film. How is it you delegate that authority to the Inspector?

Khan Bahadur Nawaz Muzaffar Khan: That is as regards locally produced films, it is the Secretary who examines the film. Probably I have not made it clear. As regards foreign films he keeps in touch with various cinemas here and if he finds anything objectionable he brings it to the notice of the Deputy Commissioner and the Board. He has not done it so far but that is the procedure.

Q. Under the new arrangements will he be under the orders of the Board?

A. We have not decided that yet. We approached the Police Officer if he would kindly let us have his services but we have not heard so far.

Q. If a western film is offered to you for censorship, there is nothing under the rules to prevent that? The rules require you to examine it?

A. Under Section 4 of the Cinematograph Act we could take action.

Q. That is not my point. Say an importer of a western film, instead of taking it to Bombay or Calcutta for censorship, brings it to you. Then under the rules wouldn't you personally have to examine it?

A. Yes.

Q. Therefore, if by any chance, your standard was considered to be less stringent than that of the other boards, you would be flooded with films—wouldn't you?

A. Generally we have adopted the standard of the other Boards.

Q. That does illustrate the necessity of a consistent standard throughout India?

A. Yes. As far as I can remember the Government has asked us to keep that standard in view, the standard that is employed in Bombay itself.

Q. You have a copy of the instructions to inspectors which have been issued by the boards of censors in Bombay and in Bengal?

A. Yes.

Q. And you are going to be guided by that?

A. Yes.

Q. I find from the rules of your Board that there is nothing here that distinguishes between a western film and a Punjab produced film, so far as your functions are concerned?

A. The rules read with the Act make it clear.

Q. So you don't think there is any necessity for the adoption of a different standard in the Punjab?

A. As I have already said, it is generally not required but there may be a very few cases.

Q. Now, coming to the question of instructional films I take it that your view is that Government should not undertake the manufacture of these films themselves but get it done through some private agency?

Mr. Parkinson: Yes, I am against that.

Mrs. Shah Nawaz: We say Government will have to undertake the production of films on agriculture, co-operative societies and so forth.

Q. It is not necessary even in their case for the government actually to have its own studio. Government can entrust the work to a private agency and give them definite instructions. That I take it is your view?

Mr. Parkinson: Yes.

Q. Now, you tried this in a few instances?

Khan Bahadur Nawaz Muzaffar Khan: Yes. Mr. Shorey has done a lot of work for us.

Q. Has his work given satisfaction?

A. As far as my own work is concerned, Mr. Shorey's photographic work is very satisfactory. Other portions of the work [other aspects of film making] I do not think he is so good at. He has no idea of arranging [assembling or editing] the film properly. If the Government departments have the time, the best thing for them will be to arrange the sequence and the arrangement of the film in such a way as to appeal to audiences.

Q. So, in your view, the combination of a more efficient Government system with private agency would produce ideal results?

A. Yes.

Q. Now with regard to instructional and propaganda films on public health matters for instance, do you think that different provincial governments can have different problems and different ideas about them?

A. Yes.

Q. So it will not be possible always to standardise those ideas for any central organisation which might undertake the work for the whole of India. That would not be perhaps feasible from our point of view?

A. Yes.

Q. Now you said that capital is shy. Don't you think that if Government were to entrust their work to private agency, that in itself would offer an inducement to private capital to flow in?

A. It might to a certain extent; it will increase the confidence of people.

Q. From that point of view would you recommend such a system as distinguished from a Government owned and Government run studio?

A. Yes, from that point of view.

Chairman: If there are several private agencies will you call for tenders?

A. Then I think we will choose the best.

Mr. Neogy: You complained about the unsatisfactory character of the actor and actresses that were available in the Punjab. We were assured by a high American authority in Bombay who knows a good deal about the subject that it is the Punjab which can be looked to for supplying the best material so far as what is described as the screen value of the human face goes. He has been all over India and is of opinion that it is the Punjab which could supply the best type of physical features?

A. I am a Punjabi myself, so it is not for me to say!

Q. You are not aware of your own special advantages?

A. Yes.

Mr. Coalman: Your Board has been constituted a very short time?

A. Yes.

Q. Well, in your private capacity then, do you notice any difference in the moral quality, shall we say, of the films that are now being produced as compared with those produced a few years ago?

A. I see so few. I am not competent to pass an opinion.

Q. What made me ask was that Mrs. Shah Nawaz referred to a particular film.

Mrs. Shah Nawaz: No. 'Royal Divorces' was a very good film.

Q. You said you had certain objections.

A. No. I was thinking about the 'The Merry Widow' and other modern American films.

Q. I just want to know if anybody here has any ideas [*sic*] on this particular subject?

Miss Bose: You mean, are they better or worse?

Q. Yes.

Mrs. Shah Nawaz: We think they are a little worse, some of these modern American films.

Mr. Webb: What is the object of having a Censor Board if they are improving?

Q. What I am wanting to get at is this: do you think the censorship ought to be tightened?

Mr. Webb: I think it ought to be.

Q. You think that modern conditions make it necessary for the censorship to be more on the alert than ever before?

A. Yes, I think so.

Q. What about posters? It seems to me that the poster of film is often objectionable where the film is not, the idea being to persuade the public that something objectionable or indecent is going to be shown.

Miss Bose: I can speak about posters. I have not been to the cinema but I have seen some objectionable posters. Yesterday a friend was telling me she saw such a bad poster she went to the Deputy Commissioner. He said he had seen it too and was going to stop the film from being shown.

Q. You think the posters ought to be censored too?

Both ladies: They ought to be.

Police Inspector: I may say from my knowledge in the last year or two there has been only one case where the Deputy Commissioner has objected to a poster. I have it on the file here if you care to see it.

(The poster in question was shown around the members of the Committee.)

Q. But have any of you noticed posters to which you have objected?

Many members: No, we have not.[32]

INDIAN CINEMATOGRAPH COMMITTEE INTERVIEWS (1927–28) MRS. ANSELL, ENTREPRENEUR

Oral Evidence of Mrs. A.K. ANSELL, Secretary, United Provinces Poultry Association, Lucknow, on Tuesday, the 6th December 1927

Chairman: Mrs. Ansell you are the Superintendent of the Poultry Farm?[33]

A. Yes.

Q. Where is that farm?

A. It is here in Lucknow.

Q. Did you have a film prepared here of your experiments?
A. Yes. The G.I.P. Railway authorities prepared one for me. Their Indian photographer came here with the Publicity Officer and took the photographs on our farm and prepared the film in Bombay.

Q. I suppose you had not to pay anything?
A. We did have to pay. I think Rs 800. Our government bought a copy for us. I think the G.I.P. people gave us that copy at the rate of Rs 1-8-0 per foot for the film.[34] This I think was reduced to half of the original price by the kindness of the Agent of the G.I.P. Railway. I took this film to England and also showed it at the World's Poultry Congress this year in Canada. I was told in England that the material the film was made of was not quite up-to-date. They told me that the film was made of very old-fashioned material [technically outdated material] and would not last very long. I gathered from them that the film was not quite up-to-date in finish.

Q. When was this film taken?
A. It was taken about 18 months ago.

Q. I suppose you gave free shows in Canada and in England?
A. I gave one free show to my friends in England and the other shows to the public in Canada. I took this Indian film to Canada to show what India was doing, as a contribution to the Poultry Congress of the World, because many nations were represented at this Congress.

Q. What was the general opinion about the technique of the film made here?
A. Oh, crowds came to see it and they were all extraordinarily interested in it, because they could see Indians doing the actual poultry work. My manager is a Brahmin, and to see Indians doing the work on the poultry farm interested people very much in Canada. The film depicted Indian poultry farming work, the chickens in the villages, and the villagers bringing them into towns, and so on. Yes, it interested people very much to see the Indians working and their life depicted.[35]

Q. Was it a free show?
A. I suppose people paid at the gate to see the whole exhibition, and India had a section in that exhibition. I had a

section quite as big as this room allotted to me for India. I had taken a lot of birds over, and also lot of Lucknow works of art and I got numbers [sic] of orders for Indian things. But this unkind Government would not pay my passage and I had to go at my own expense.

Q. You think that such sort of films would interest the people in England and Canada or America?

A. I think if you prepared films here to show in the West, they would be a great draw.

Q. Do you mean as regards scenery and life?

A. Yes. All sorts of Indian scenes. If you prepare good films over here and show them in the West, they will, I think bring in far more money because the audience there can afford to go to cinemas. Here very few can afford even 4 or 8 annas for a seat.

Q. Have you seen 'The Light of Asia'?

A. No.

Q. Have you seen any Indian films here?

A. No. I have not seen any here, but I have seen some in Calcutta. I am afraid I very seldom go to the cinemas.

Q. Did you show your film to the ordinary public here?

A. It has been shown free at many railway stations in the third class waiting rooms. It has also been shown to the public in Calcutta in the Eden Gardens.[36]

Q. Were you present at any of these shows?

A. Yes.

Q. Did ordinary people follow it all right?

A. Oh, yes.

Q. Were they able to understand it all or not?

A. Of course; they enjoyed seeing the life, the action of the birds and so on.

Q. Do you think they obtained some benefit from attending it?

A. I think so. And I have titles in Urdu so that they can follow what it means.[37]

Q. You see yesterday we were told that the people here do not understand these films and that it was not much use showing them the films.

A. Well, I do think that illiterate people as yet understand very little because if you show a photograph they do not know which way up it is. But that will all come in time. The more you show them the more they will understand. That is one of the best ways of educating them, isn't it?

Q. You believe it will help in educating the masses here?

A. Simple films, not complicated films. And films about their own industries and their own life, thought out very carefully as to what would appeal to them, prepared [made] by your own people who know how they think.

Q. You think that will [be] a useful thing?

A. I should say it will be a most useful thing. One of the most valuable ways of teaching.

Q. On hygiene, public health, and so on.[38]

A. And all the cottage industries.

Q. And you would advocate Government spending money in such directions?

A. I would, provided the films are prepared carefully, not from a scientific point of view. They want to be very carefully thought out so that they may appeal to the villager. I should say if we could only go on lorries and take the cinemas to the villagers that would bring great joy to the villagers. Travelling lorries: [*sic*] Because I don't think they can afford to pay money in coming to the theatres. I think that the theatres must be a loss to many people who are running them. In England the seats are so extraordinarily cheap compared to what they are here. There, a workman has to spend only 3d [pence] or 4d [pence] to go to the cinema, which means only 2 annas practically. Here it is 4 annas which is a lot of money for the people here, for an amusement of that sort.

Q. Have you any experience of children's education?

A. Well, of course only at home. I have children coming to my films here but I have not any experience.

Colonel Crawford: I have one question. Have your films of poultry breeding interested the villagers. Have you shown it to the villagers at all?

A. Not exactly *in* the villages, but *to* the villagers who come into the big district fairs.

Q. Do you think it interests them?

A. They follow the movement of it and I think they realise that I am trying to show them bigger and better fowls. I should say they don't understand it all, they could not. My film has to be a film that appeals to the educated as well.

Q. But you think they recognise that they are fowls?

A. Oh, yes, they crow and make all sorts of noises like the birds do when they are watching the film.

Q. We had a witness yesterday who said that they could not even understand what it was.

A. I think animal life they understand, on account of the movement in it.

Q. How was your film made up? It simply shows different sizes of fowls?

A. Oh no, it shows the farm starting in the morning, and all the work of the day, the laying of the eggs, how the chickens come out in incubators and how they grow.

Q. Do you think they understood?

A. Oh yes, we explained in Urdu, for instance, 'this is the machine which hatches the eggs'. That they see, the drawer of the machine being full of eggs.

Q. Do you think they can follow?

A. I think they do to a certain extent. They are extraordinarily interested. They think I am sort of a magic person who produces chicken in half an hour.

Mr. Green. You told us this film cost Rs 800. Can you tell us what length it was?

A. Yes, it was 1,700 feet.

Q. You told us that simple films would certainly be appreciated, that we should at any rate not start with giving them other than simple films. Would you be prepared to take the view that for such simple films a commercial agency is hardly possible?

A. ...But I should say that none of these educational films can possibly pay really.

Q. Oh no, I didn't mean that. I was wondering whether the same agency which prepares commercial films would be able to prepare simple films.

A. Yes, because we should employ people who thoroughly understood [*sic*] the art of making films from the technical side.

Sir Haroon Jaffer: Why did you put on those titles in Urdu also? Why not in Pusthu?[39]

A. Because Urdu is the language of the province.

Q. Because it is better understood in the province? Of course Hindi would be. You would prefer Hindustani for these films so that the illiterate and other people might understand?

A. You see the G.I.P. people who prepared the film did not give me the titles in Urdu; they gave them to me only in English and I had to have them made by some Meerut firm—a Muhammadan translated the titles for me and these titles are shown separately, in addition to the English titles.

Q. You think that if such films are shown with the Hindustani titles they will be appreciated better by people all over India?

A. I should say so because they pride themselves on reading and they would spell it out—it would help to teach them to read also.

Q. You show these films free?

A. Yes.

Q. You think they are appreciated? Suppose you charge one pice or two pice, don't you think they will be more appreciated? People do not care to see what they are shown free.

A. It might be so. My show is a free thing. I don't know what I should do with the money, or how I should collect it.

Q. But would they care to come and see your films if you show them free?

A. Oh yes, the theatres where I have shown them were always full, absolutely packed.

Chairman: You have shown them in the theatres also?

A. Yes. At a Meerut theatre, and at Aligarh in the theatre at the fair. In the town in the big Meerut theatre.

Sir Haroon Jaffer: You showed this in America you said just now?

A. I showed them in Ottawa, the capital city of Canada.

Q. Didn't your poultry industry benefit in any way?

A. Oh, yes, because I brought back a great many orders for Asil, or Indian fighting birds, as well as for Indian works of art. And letters are coming every mail asking me to find similar Indian birds to send across the sea.

Q. Then it is very good to show these films in other parts of the Empire.

A. Certainly. I am having orders every mail.

Q. Do you think that if Canada or Australia send such films here they will be appreciated?

A. I should think so, very much by the educated people. Not by the masses as yet.

Sir Haroon Jaffer: In which part of Lucknow is your farm?

A. It is out at Dilkusha. I think you might care to come and see it.

Q. Well, if we can find the time we will try and come.

A. Yes please do so. I am going to Calcutta to-morrow [*sic*] morning to a big poultry show for All India there, and I shall be away, but my manager will be at the farm and he will show you everything.

NOTES

1　For 'procedure and findings', see Priya Jaikumar, *Cinema at the End of Empire: A Politics of Transition in Britain and India* (Duke University Press, 2006).

2　Kaushik Bhaumik, 'Sulochana: Clothes, Stardom and Gender in Early Indian Cinema', in *Fashioning Film Stars, Dress, Culture, Identity*, edited by Rachel Moseley (London: BFI Publishing, 2005): 88–97.

3　Neepa Majumdar, *Wanted Cultured Ladies Only!, Female Stardom and Cinema in India, 1930s–1950s* (New Delhi: Oxford University Press, 2010).

4   Debashree Mukherjee has also written about female actors of the late colonial period, in *Marg*, 62: 54–65, 4 June 2011.

5   An extract from *Indian Cinematograph Committee Report*, Volume 1: 213 and Volume 5: 1–7. The Report is presented as in the original.

6   This part of the interview was recorded on camera, Saturday 12 November 1927.

7   Despite being the icon of cosmopolitanism, it is evident from her interviews (and as shown by Neepa Majumdar, 2010) that Sulochana gradually became the 'respectable lady'. Moreover, her interviews on one hand show her own dilemma, on the other, it also disturbs any linear reading of the lives and works of female actors.

8   See Ratan Bai's letters in Chapter 2.

9   The term picture-play was fairly common during this time, primarily because in several cases, especially in Calcutta, theatrical performances were regularly recorded and shown in the theatres. The other popular names were Bioscope and Talkies. For instance, *Chitrapanji* (Kartik, 1341 [November 1934], 4(1): presented a list of hundred names for the new deity or the 'Beautiful Talkie'. The write-up included a list of hundred names for the talkies in alphabetical order. Therefore, the suggested names were as follows: 'Actorgraph', 'Audicine', 'Audima', 'Audio play', 'Audio picture', 'Cinelog', 'Cinemaphone', 'Dicodrama', 'Filmotalk', 'Phonofilm', 'Phonoplay', 'Photophone', 'Phonie', 'Pictalk', 'Movietalk' 'Motiotone', 'Movieplay', 'Oral films', Oratone', 'Seephonie', 'Screen show', 'Sono film', 'Sound movies', Spekie', 'Talk art', 'Talkie', 'View tone', 'View Voice', 'Visatone', 'Vitaphone', 'Vocal film', 'Zono tone', etc.

10 Note in her previous interview she mentions that before joining films she 'was in the telephone office'.

11 However, the industry was crowded with Eurasian actors, and especially stunt queen Nadia, of Wadia Movietone, would have a long career until the fifties. See Valentina Vitali, *Hindi Action Cinema: Industries, Narratives, Bodies* (Oxford University Press, 2008).

12 The popular actor Dhiren Ganguly from Bengal (2, 642), said the following to the ICC:

Q. You are a director?

A. Yes.

Q. You are a director, or an actor too?

A. I acted myself in the role part once. [I acted once].

Q. You both act and direct others to act?

A. Yes.

Q. I suppose you began merely as an amateur; you did not get any training?

A. Yes I have published many books. 'Expression and Caricatures'. *The Times of India* and all papers have published my expressions.

Q. That is all right. But you never took any training for film direction?

A. No.

13   Popularly described as the father of Indian cinema, D.G. Phalke (3: 869–85) said the following to the same committee, regarding the international screenings of his films:

Q. Do you think if you improve the quality of Indian film you will have a wider market abroad? Do you think well made Indian film will command a good audience if shown in England?

A. Not the present ones produced in India, but well made ones may audience, I have exhibited some of my own films in England in London such as *Savitri, Harishchandra,* and other films and the press in London remarked, 'From the technical point of view Phalke's films are excellent'.

Q. Did you make money in England by the exhibition of your films there?

A. No.

A. I did not do it in a commercial way.

Chairman: You did not try to market your films there?

A. No.

Q. Why did you not do so if you found your films attractive there?

A. I had not sufficient working capital with me to do so. As a matter there was a big demand for my films. They asked for 25 and 30 copies of the same. It was then that I formed the Hindustan Film Company.

Q. Do you think if you can get sufficient capital you

can produce films in India which will command an international market?

A. Yes, I do think so.

Mr. Green: I should like to be able to agree with you...

Q. You said you sent your films to Singapore. Had you success there?

A. Yes, it was a success. We have sent films to Singapore, Rangoon and other places.

Q. Have you ever tried to send your films to...Africa?

A. Yes, we have sent some of our films to Zanzibar.

14 See Jamuna Barua's interview and Kananbala's writing (Chapter 1).

15 In his testimony, D. G. Ganguly replied the following in response to the queries:

Q. You made money over it?

A. Yes.

Q. On all these pictures you have made money?

A. Yes.

Q. How many weeks did they run?

A. Three weeks continuously run here, and in Bombay we sold it for Rs 22,000 to K. D. Das [director and producer of *Jamai Babu*, the only surviving silent film from Bengal].

Mr. Green: What did it cost you to produce?

A. Some Rs 19,000–20,000.

Q. And you sold the Bombay rights alone for Rs 22,000?

A. Yes.

Chairman: And it ran for three months here?

A. Yes, continually. And after that we sold it to the Madan Theatres who now have it.

And Phalke said the following regarding production costs:

Q. How much do you spend oil an average film at present, approximately?

A. Say, about 10,000 rupees.

Q. And you get a good return on that investment. I suppose?

A. Yes.

Q. How long does it take you to recover the money laid out on each film?

A. Generally a film should last not least for 4 months,

but sometimes they are spoiled swig to bad operation and bad machines within 3 or 4 weeks.

Q. And therefore you have to make more copies, I suppose?

A. Yes. The usual projection speed should he [*sic*] about 3 to 4 thousand feet per hour but sometimes the projectors even show about 8 to 10 thousand feet per hour with the result the film is easily spoiled ...

Q. What is the amount that one can spend on the production of one film with a reasonable hope of getting back an adequate return?

A. Not more than Rs 25,000 per subject.

Q. Do you think you can produce a first-class film on that amount?

A. Yes, after a time.

Q. You are therefore pinning your faith on the matter of expert technique and training?

A. Yes.

Q. It is not a question of having to use a good deal of money in payment to first-class actors and actress or improved scenes?

A. No, I don't think so. With a capital of Rs 25,000 I can produce a first-class film.

Q. You can get a profit also?

A. Yes.

16 In my article, 'Of Bhadromahila, Blouses, and "Bustofine": Re-viewing Bengali High Culture (1930s–40s) from a Low Angle' in Clara Sarmento and Ricardo Campos et al. eds., *Popular and Visual Culture: Design, Circulation and Consumption* (Cambridge: Cambridge Scholars Publishing, 2014), I discuss the ways in which dress and costume of female actors were gradually fitted into the bhadromahila framework.

17 This interview was held on Monday 19 December 1927; ICCR, 2: 895–97.

18 Himanshu Rai (ICCR 3: 998–1015) the actor, director and producer of the film said the following before the committee:

Q. Yon [*sic*] were the Chief [*sic*] actor in 'The Light of Asia'? In the part Buddha?

A. Yes.

Q. I suppose all the actors and actresses were Indians?
A. Yes, they were all recruited from India.
Q. One of them was Anglo-Indian?
A. Yes, the girl who took the lending part [*sic*] was an Anglo-Indian. She appeared as Sita Devi.
Q. That was the first time she assumed that name?
A. Yes
Sir Haroon Jaffer [ICC member]: Is she one of those we have seen?
A. Her name is Dyer. [?] I believe.
Chairman: We have seen her.
Mr. Green [ICC member]: That very young girl?
A. Yes.
Chairman: Who recruited the actresses?
A. I did.
Q. Are they fairly respectable people?
A. So far as I know all of them were respectable.
Q. Did you find any difficulty in getting them to join?
A. Very much.
Q. I suppose the actors also were from a respectable class of people?
A. Yes, when I say actors I mean the principal actresses and actors.
Q. You took them from Bombay and Bengal?
A. Some were from Madras, and some from Bengal. Some from Hyderabad.
A. Some were Parsees and also there were two Madrasi Hindu ladies.

19 See Sabita Devi's article anthologized here (Chapter 2).
20 Note eminent actor, dancer, choreographer and 'social lady' Sadhana Bose's memoir narrates similar journeys into cinema. However, Sadhana Bose was the granddaughter of the nineteenth-century social reformer Kesab Chandra Sen. See Sadhana Bose, *Silpir Atmakatha* (Kolkata: Pratibhash, 2012).
21 Also see interviews with Jamuna Barua (Chapter 2) and Sulochana (referred to earlier in this chapter).
22 Emelka Studios distributed the film across Europe and later it was traded with the well-known production house Pathe.

23 See *Sonar Daag* for narratives of such journeys.

24 This is an extract from ICCR, 2: 1–14, taken from the interviews of the Punjab [Province] Board of Film Censors. The report of ICC gives a detailed list of the films not issued under the censor certificate.

25 See Madhuja Mukherjee. ed. *Aural Films, Oral Cultures, Essays on Cinema from the Early Sound Era* (Kolkata: Jadavpur University Press, 2012).

26 See Colonial Film Archive.

27 See J. J. Madan's testimonies in ICCR (2) for a discussion on the types of American films, which were imported to India.

28 See Sita Devi's interview redrafted here. Also see Himanshu Rai testimony in ICCR (3). Rai and Osten produced a trilogy— *Light of Asia* (1925, on Buddha's life), *Shiraz* (1928, about the Taj Mahal) and *A Throw of Dice* (on the gambling kings from the *Mahabharata*); also see Priya Jaikumar, 'A Throw of Dice (*Prapancha Pash*), Review', *Modernism/Modernity* 16, 4 (2009): 845–48; Priya Jaikumar, 'More than Morality: The Indian Cinematograph Committee Interviews (1927)', *The Moving Image* 3, 1 (Spring 2003) 82–100.

29 K. A. Abbas, the journalist from *Bombay Chronicle* and a columnist from *Film India*, would regularly write about Soviet Russia and the urgency of education films.

30 *The Indian Cinematograph Year Book* (1938) published an entire list of cinemas in India. ICCR (4) provides a list of cinemas as well.

31 Also see Someswar Bhowmik, *Cinema and Censorship, The Politics of Control in India* (New Delhi: Orient Blackswan, 2009).

32 The asterisk mark in the beginning of this level head has been retained as it appears in the original. The related note in the original is reproduced here: [In the case of those whose names are marked with an asterisk the record of oral evidence was not corrected by the witness.]

33 ICCR 2: 375–79.

34 The price is stated as it appears in the original.

35 See Colonial Film Archive.

36 Tent bioscope was extremely popular during the early phase and in the silent era. Pashupati Chattopadhyay writes (in Banglar Cinema Shiplo', *Batayan*, September 1932, pp.15–19),

The tent-bioscope on the very first day of its inaugural was faced with an obstacle. A game of destiny! On the designated day, the sky broke loose on Kolkata and there was torrential rain throughout the day. Only five or six people arrived amidst the water clogged condition to watch 'bioscope'. And, they viewed the show. The Sahib [J. J. Madan] was told that the place is not at all conducive, since this is what has happened on the very first day! After listening to these words he smiled, and said that, on such a calamitous day when the crows and vultures dare not to fly, six people had come to view the show, spending their own money. This place will reap gold.

This description of a nascent viewing culture, which is deeply connected to our local history, becomes significant as we look back into the narratives of Kolkata cinemas, and reconsider the notes on the show houses.

37 During the silent era, it was a common practice to change the language of the inter-tiles according to the specific sector.

38 See the Colonial Film Archive, the Colonial Film Database and the Centre of South Asian Studies Film Archive for a series of public health and remedial films.

39 Also known as Pashto, the language of the Pathans. Urdu at that time was perceived as being more sophisticated.

EPILOGUE:
WHO IS BADAR BEGUM?

Until very recently I did not know about Badar Begum. Yet, as a child in the eighties—at the time when Doordarshan was involved in promoting state-funded art cinema—I had watched M. S. Sathyu's *Garam Hawa* (1973) on television, and was moved by the plot, and processes of image making have stayed with me, I believe. Years later as a student of cinema, I was marvelled by the handling of complex plot elements like partition, marginalization of the minority community, issues of culture, politics, love, gender, labour and memory. The architecture of places—houses, streets, and offices—mapped an extremely complicated terrain of India's political and social history. Curiously, eventually when I met M. S. Sathyu in a seminar in FTII, Pune, as late as 2007, he narrated the following story. Certainly, I could be mixing up things in terms of the details; nonetheless, the crux of the story is indeed a fact.

Apparently, Sathyu was hunting for a mansion to shoot *Garam Hawa*. One night, he visited an old deserted house in a certain

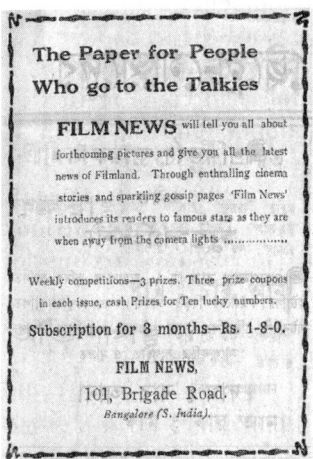

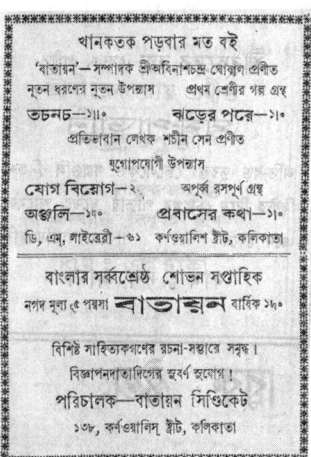

Cinema within the contested public sphere

city (Agra) in North India. It was seemingly a 'house of public women'. An elderly, ravaged looking woman opened the doors and insisted that the house was unmanned. While Sathyu did not like the house he actually loved the woman. He wished to cast her as the old woman/mother in *Garam Hawa*. However, Sathyu was unsure if she would or could act at all. Eventually, not only the woman agreed to act in his film; she disclosed that she always wanted to be an actor. Sometime during the early phase (the twenties) of Indian cinema, Badar Begum had travelled to Bombay/Mumbai to look for work. In the process she was abused and exploited and after such violent encounters with cinema she returned to her city and worked as a 'public woman' of sorts. Yet, at a very late stage in her life, such an opportunity knocked at her door. Later, *Garam Hawa* received a national award and produced one of the most remarkable moments in the history of cinema. For instance, while the family (especially her son) decides to vacate the mansion and shift to another place, the old mother as thin as a waif curls up like a worm underneath a covering, cries and refuses to leave her ancestral home.

Badar Begum's memorable performance and her life tell us a very complicated history of the nation and the state of the film industry. Moreover, her life is an inspiring story that speaks about the doggedness of dreams

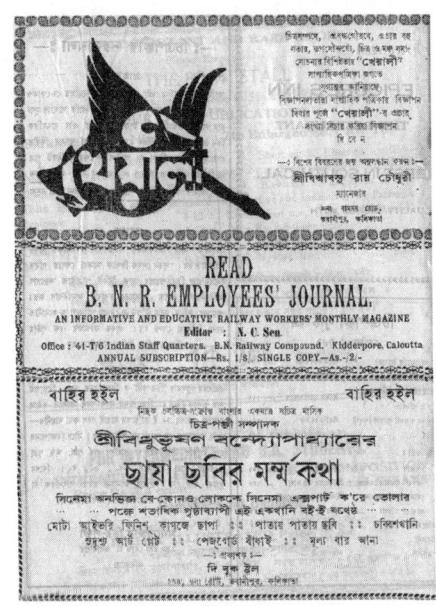

Kheyali, *one of the popular magazines of the period*

Epilogue: Who Is Badar Begum?

and the irony of it. Her life also throws light on the lives of many such actors who struggled, earned through disparate means, and sometimes eventually, became beggars like Kolkata's Nirada Sundari discussed earlier, or vanished into nothingness like Ratan Bai. Badar Begum was an actor who dreamt of cinema, and may be described as the embodiment of the history of Indian cinemas. Badar Begum and many such working women actually went on to produce our film history. This book negotiates such narrations to *re-tell* the tale, and interrogate the theoretical frameworks of writing film history.

BIBLIOGRAPHY

Periodicals, Journals, Reports

Ababhash (Bengali): 2005
Amrita Bazar Patrika: 1941–42
American Cinematographer: 1932
Ananda Bazaar Patrika: 1940–45
Batayan (Bengali): 1932
Bioscope (Bengali): 1930
Chitralekha (Bengali): 1930–31
Chitrapanji (Bengali): 1932–38
Chitrapat (Hindi): 1932–33
Cinema Sansar (Hindi): 1932–33
Dipali (Bengali): 1931–32
Filmfare: 1965–66
Film India: 1935–45
Filmland: 1931–32
Film World: 1934
ICC Report: 1927–28
Journal of Motion Picture Society of India: 1932–36
Journal of the Moving Image: 1999 onwards.
JugaPat (Bengali): 2004.
Kheyali (Bengali): 1932
Motion Picture Herald: 1946
Nachghar (Bengali): 1926–27
New Cinema Sansar: 1933
Rangbhoomi (Hindi): 1933
Sight and Sound: 1935 onwards
Talk-A-Tone: 1939–1944
Varieties Weekly: 1933–34

Books and Articles

Abbas, K. A. 1941 (August). 'Educating India's 400 Millions, Harness the Movies to Build a Nation'. In *Film India*: 58–60.
———.1939. 'About Nothing....'. In *Film India*. November: 29 and 64.

Anderson, Benedict. 1991. *Imagined Communities, Reflections on the Origin and Spread of Nationalism*. London, New York: Verso.

Bagchi, Amiya. 1972. *Private Investment in India*, 1900–1939. Cambridge: Cambridge University Press.

Balibar, Etienne, and Immanuel Wallerstein. 1991. *Race, Nation, Class: Ambiguous Identities*. London: Verso.

Bandopadhyay, Samik (ed.). 1993. *Indian Cinema: Contemporary Perceptions from the Thirties*. Jamshepur: Celluloid Chapter.

Barnouw, Eric, and S. Krishnaswamy. 1980. *Indian Film* (Second edition). New Delhi: Oxford University Press.

Barua, Pramathesh. 1934 (January). 'A Problem'. In *Varieties Weekly, Varieties Annual*: 32.

Bhabha, Homi (ed.). 1999. *Nation and Narration*. London, New York: Routledge.

Bhowmik, S. 1995. *Indian Cinema, Colonial Contours*. Calcutta: Papyrus.

Berger, John. 1972. *Ways of Seeing*. London: BBC and Penguin Books.

Burra, Rani (ed.). 1981. *Looking Back–1896–1960*. New Delhi: The Directorate of Film Festivals.

Brooks, Peter. 1987. *The Melodramatic Imagination, Balzac, Henry James, Melodrama and the Mode of Excess*. New Haven: Yale University Press. (Originally published in 1976).

Chakrabarty, Dipesh. 2001. *Provincializing Europe, Postcolonial Thought and Historical Difference*. New Delhi: Oxford University Press.

Chakravarty, Sumita S. 1993. *National Identity in Indian Popular Cinema*, 1947-87. New Delhi: Oxford University Press.

Chandra, Bipan. 1979. *Nationalism and Colonialism in Modern India*. New Delhi: Orient Longman.

Chatterjee, Partha. 2002. *The Partha Chatterjee Omnibus*. New Delhi: Oxford University Press.

Chaudhuri, Sukanta (ed.). 2005. *Calcutta, The Living City*, vols. 1 and 2. New Delhi: Oxford University Press. (First published in 1990.)

Dissanayake, Wimal (ed.). 1993. *Melodrama and Asian Cinema*. New York: Cambridge University Press.

Gledhill, Christine (ed.). 1987. *Home Is Where the Heart Is: Studies in Melodrama and the Women's Film*. London: BFI Publishing.

Guha, Ranajit. 1988. *An Indian Historiography of India: A Nineteenth-Century Agenda and Its Implications.* Calcutta/New Delhi: for CSSS; Calcutta: K.P. Bagchi and Company.

Gooptu, Sharmistha. 2010. *Bengali Cinema: An Other Nation.* New Delhi: Lotus Collection; Roli Books.

Habermas, Jurgen. 1989. *The Structural Transformation of the Public Sphere: An Inquiry into a Category of Bourgeois Society* (Thomas Burger, Trans.). Great Britain: Polity Press.

Jha, B. 1990. *B.N. Sircar: A Monograph.* Calcutta: NFAI, Pune, in association with Seagull Books.

Kaarsholm, Preben (ed.), 2002. 'City Flicks, Cinema, Urban Worlds and Modernities in India and Beyond', Occasional Paper, no.22, Roskilde University, Denmark.

Kaviraj, Sudipta. 1995. *Unhappy Consciousness: Bankim Chandra Chattopadhyay and the Formation of Nationalist Discourse in India.* New Delhi: Oxford University Press.

Landy, Marcia. (ed.). 2001. *The Historical Film: History and Memory in Media.* London: The Athlone Press.

Misra, B.B. 1978. *The Indian Middle Classes, Their Growth in Modern Times.* New Delhi: Oxford University Press. (Originally published in 1961).

Niranjana, T. et al. 1993. *Interrogating Modernity, Culture and Colonialism in India.* Calcutta: Seagull.

Orsini, Francesca. 2002. *The Hindi Public Sphere (1920–1940), Language and Literature in the Age of Nationalism.* New Delhi: Oxford University Press.

Prasad, M. Madhava. 1998. *Ideology of the Hindi Film: A Historical Reconstruction.* Delhi: OUP.

Raha, Kiranmoy. 1995. *Bengali Cinema.* Calcutta: Nandan.

Rajadhyaksha, Ashish. 1994. 'Viewer's View'. In *Light of Asia: Indian Silent Cinema, 1912–1934* Suresh Chabria, Paolo Cherchi Usai (eds). New Delhi: Wiley Eastern Ltd.

———. 1987. 'The Phalke Era, Conflict of Traditional Form and Modern Technology'. In *Journal of Arts and Ideas.* 14–15.

Rajadhyaksha, Ashish and Paul Willemen (eds). 1999. *Encyclopaedia of Indian Cinema* (Second edition). New York: Oxford University Press.

Ramachandran, T. M. (ed.). 1985. *Seventy Years of Indian Cinema,* 1913–1983. Bombay: Cinema India International.

Sarkar, Sumit. 1997. *Writing Social History.* New Delhi: Oxford University Press.

———. 1987. *Bengal 1928–1934, Politics of Protests.* New Delhi: Oxford University Press.

———. 1984. *Modern India, 1885–1947.* New Delhi: Macmillan India Ltd.

Sarkar, Tanika. 2001. *Hindu Wife, Hindu Nation.* New Delhi: Permanent Black.

Vasudevan, Ravi (ed.). 2000. *Making Meaning in Indian Cinema.* New Delhi: Oxford University Press.

Vitali, Valentina. 2008. *Hindi Action Cinema, Industries, Narrtives, Bodies.* New Delhi: Oxford University Press.

Books in Bengali

Bankim Rachana Sangraha. 1973. Calcutta: Sakharata Prakashan, Pashchim Bongo Nirokhorata Durikaran Samiti: 1, 1.

Chakraborty, Pinaki. 2006. *Chalachitrer Itihashe New Theatres.* Calcutta: ABP.

Ghosh, Debiprasad (ed.). 1991. *Bangla Bhashaye Chalachitra Charcha,* 1923-33. Calcutta: Cine Club of Calcutta.

Ghosh, Gouranga Prasad. 1982. *Sonar Daag.* Calcutta: Jogomaya Prakashani.

Mitra, Nandan (ed.). 2006. *Bangla Chalachitrer Bikashe Pramathesh Barua.* Kolkata: Chalachitra O Sanskriti Charcha Kendro.

Mukhopadhyay, Kalish. 1962. *Bangla Chalachitra Shilper Itihas, 1897–1947.* Calcutta: Rupamancha.

Shanyal, Amiya. 2004. *New Theatres Smarane.* Calcutta: Kolkata Book Fair.